HORROR ANIME COLORING BOOK

by TONY CLARK

This Coloring Book Belongs to

____

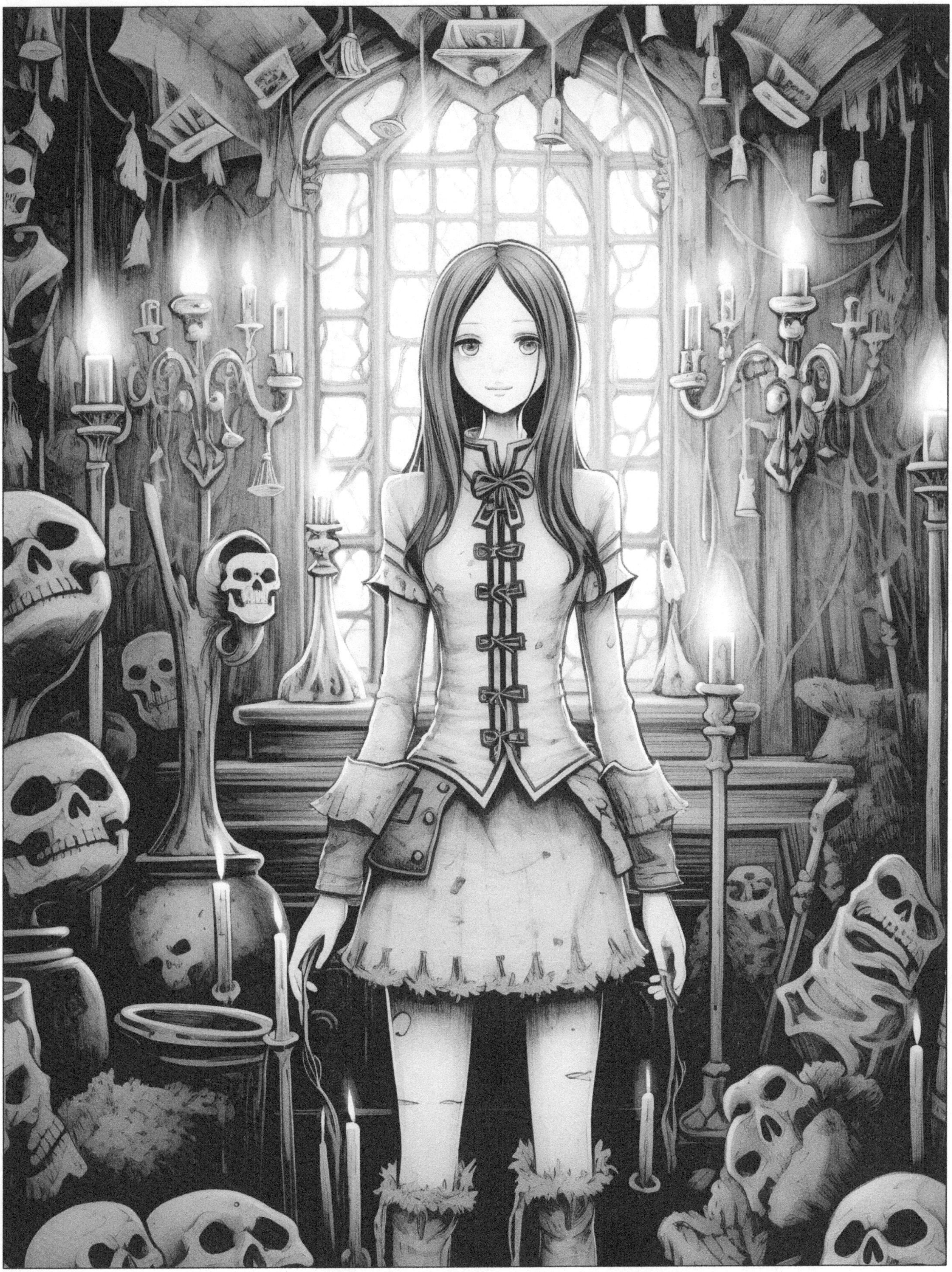

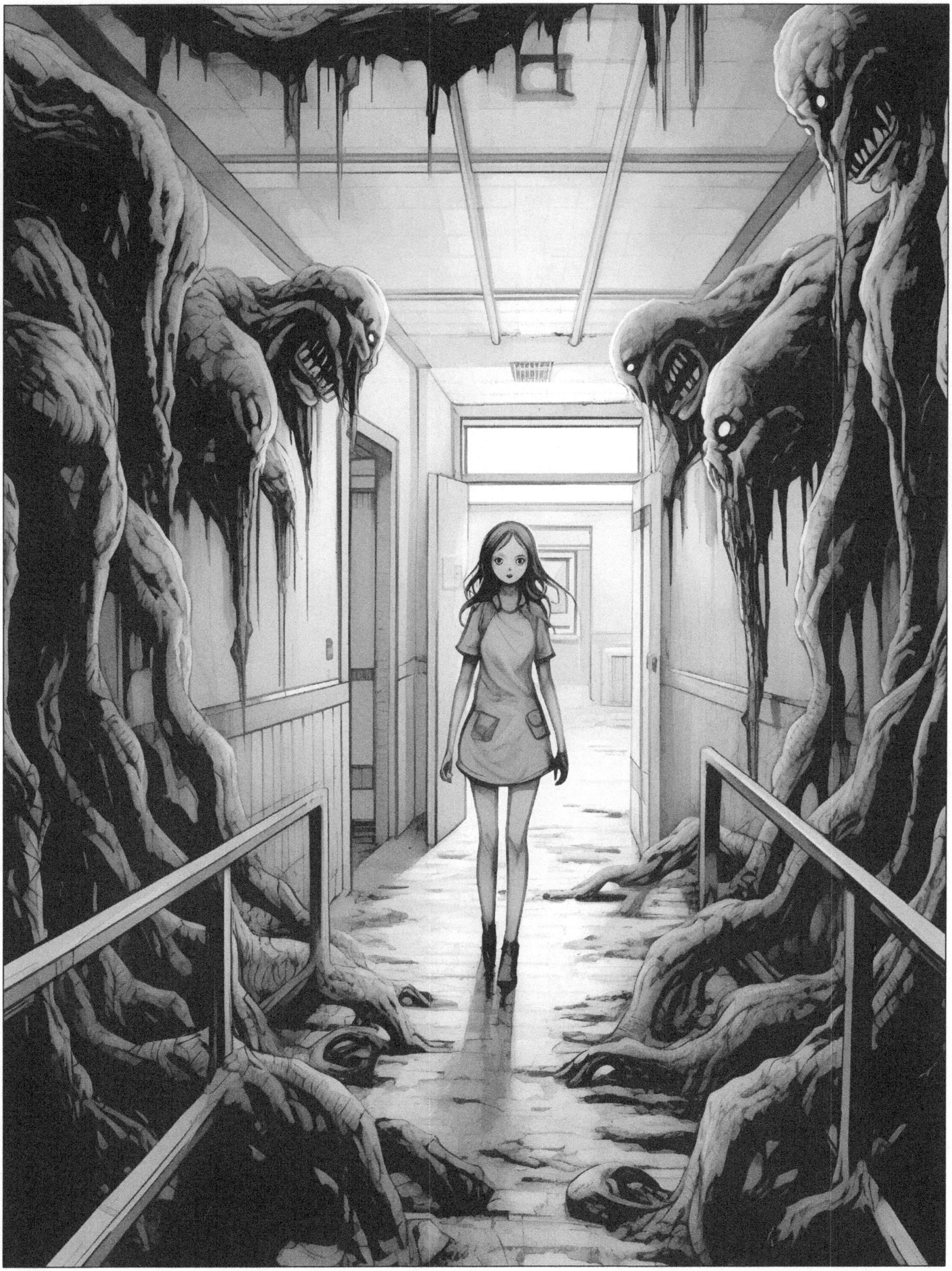

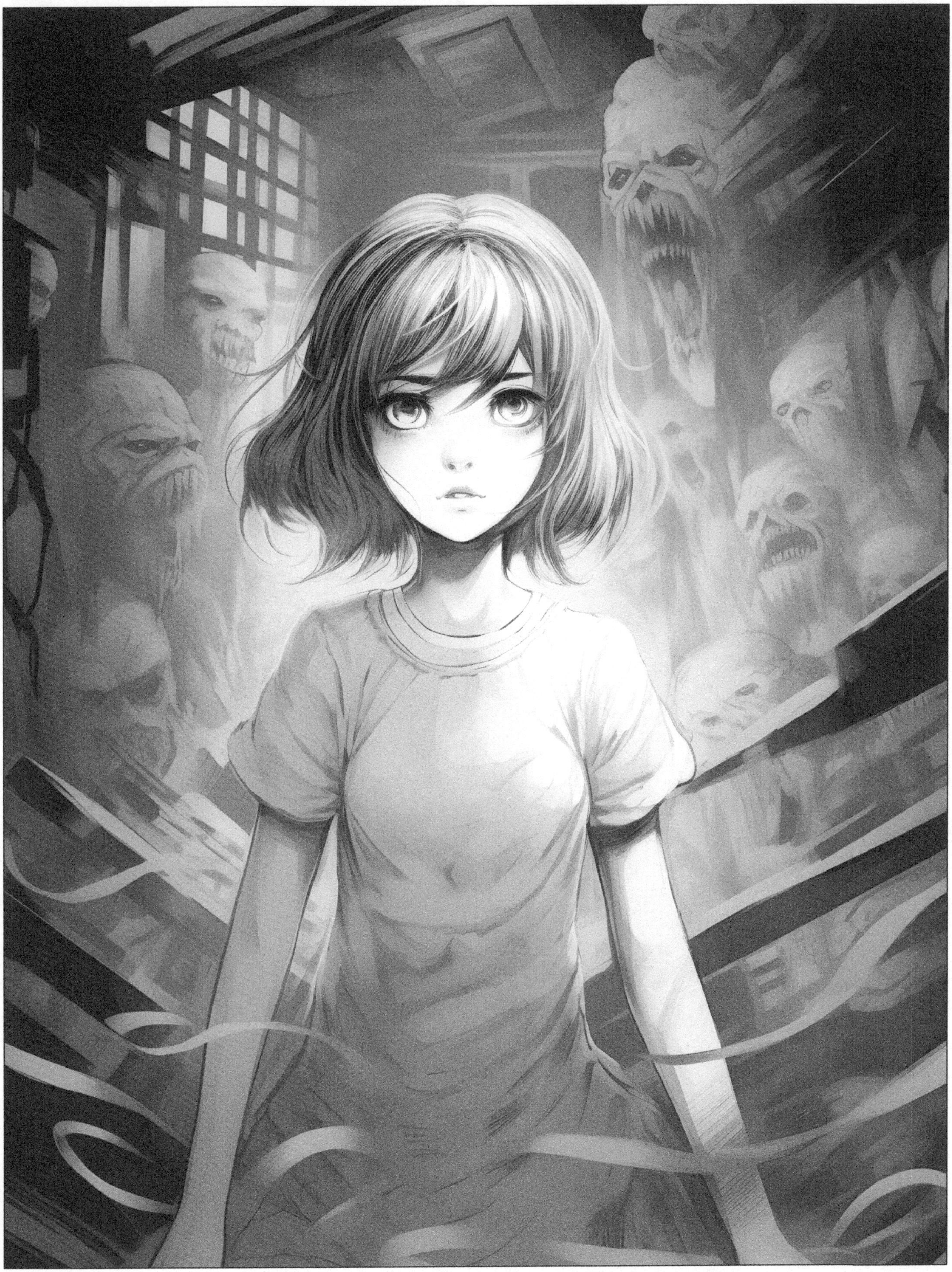

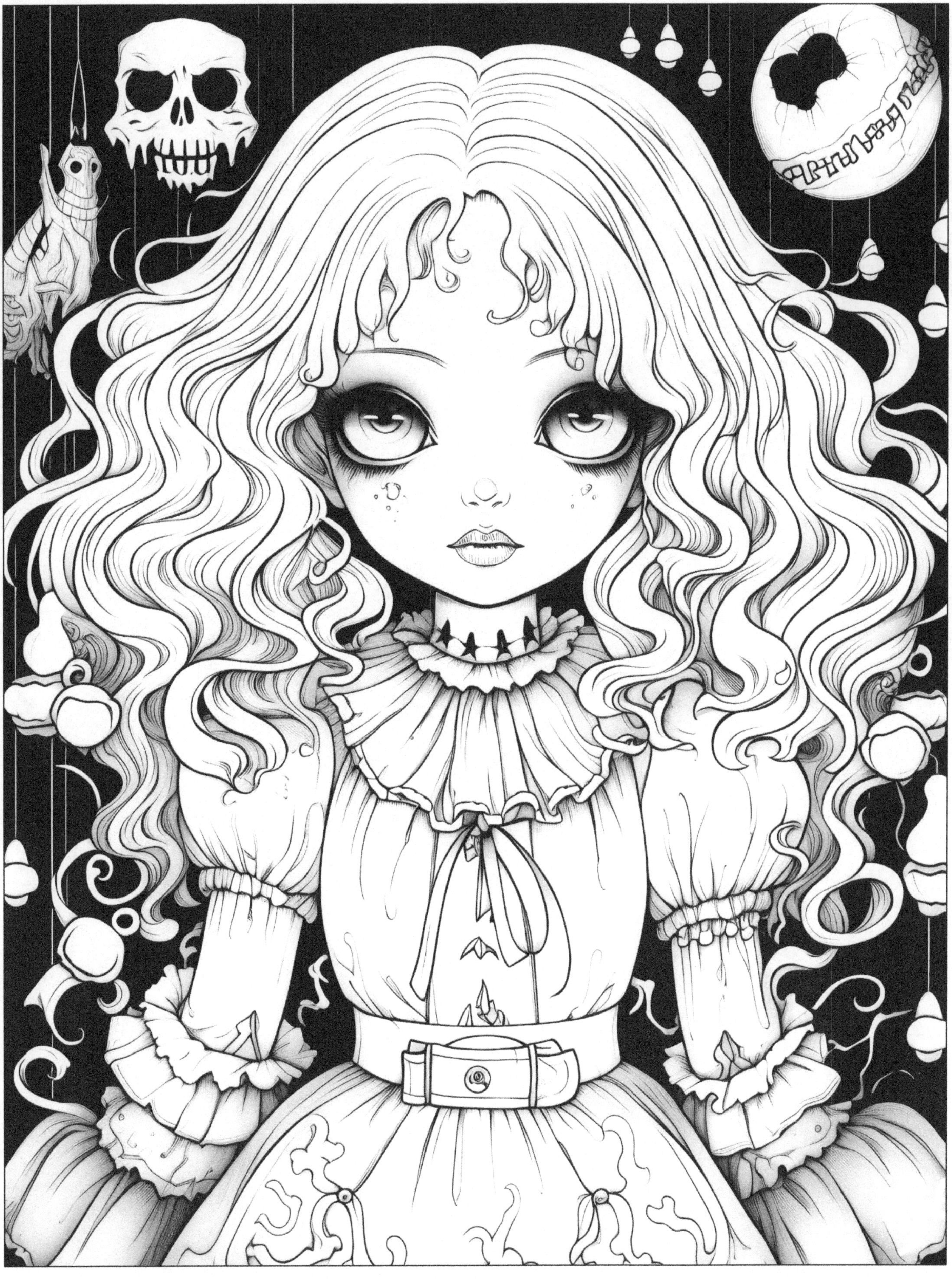

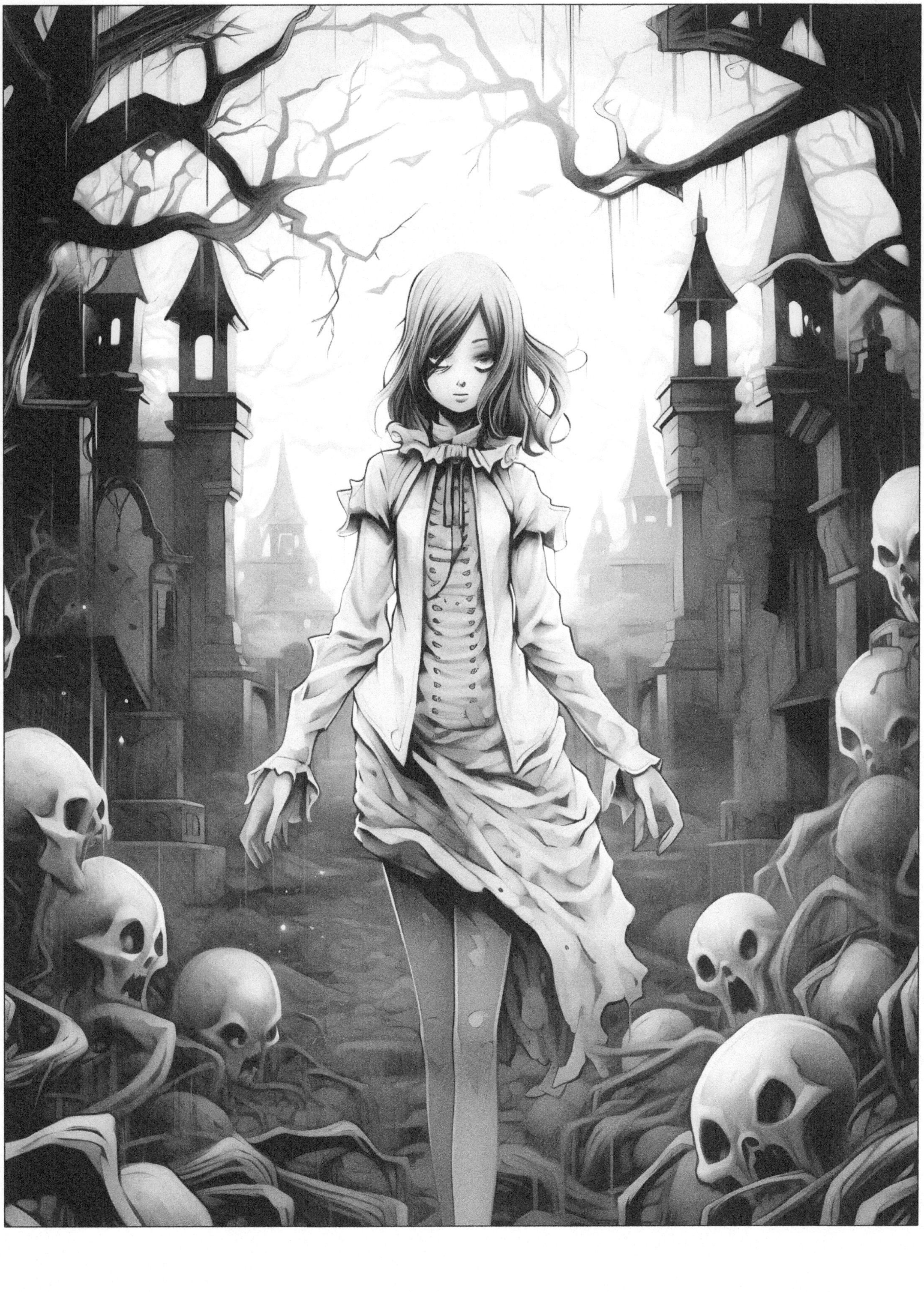

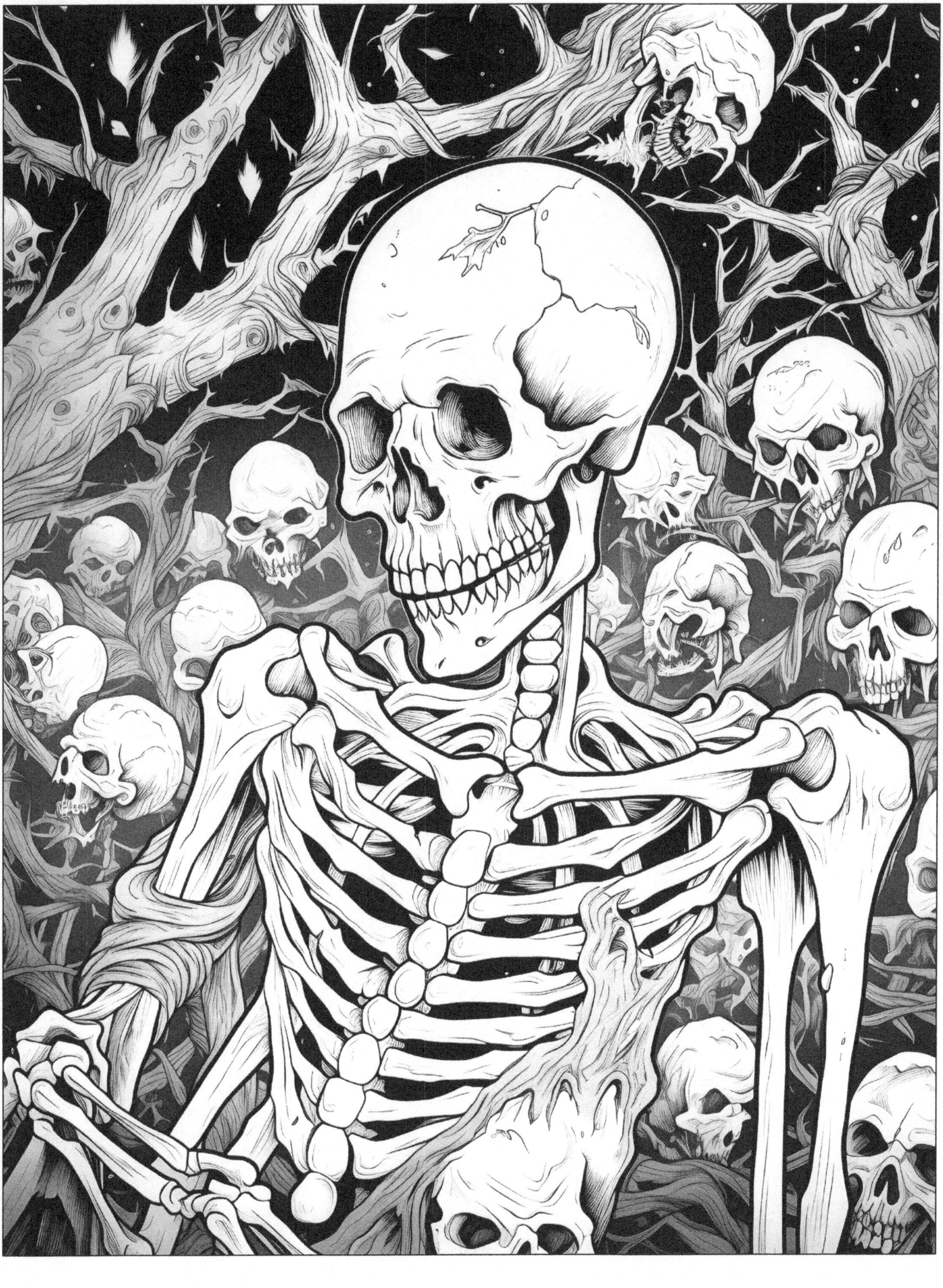

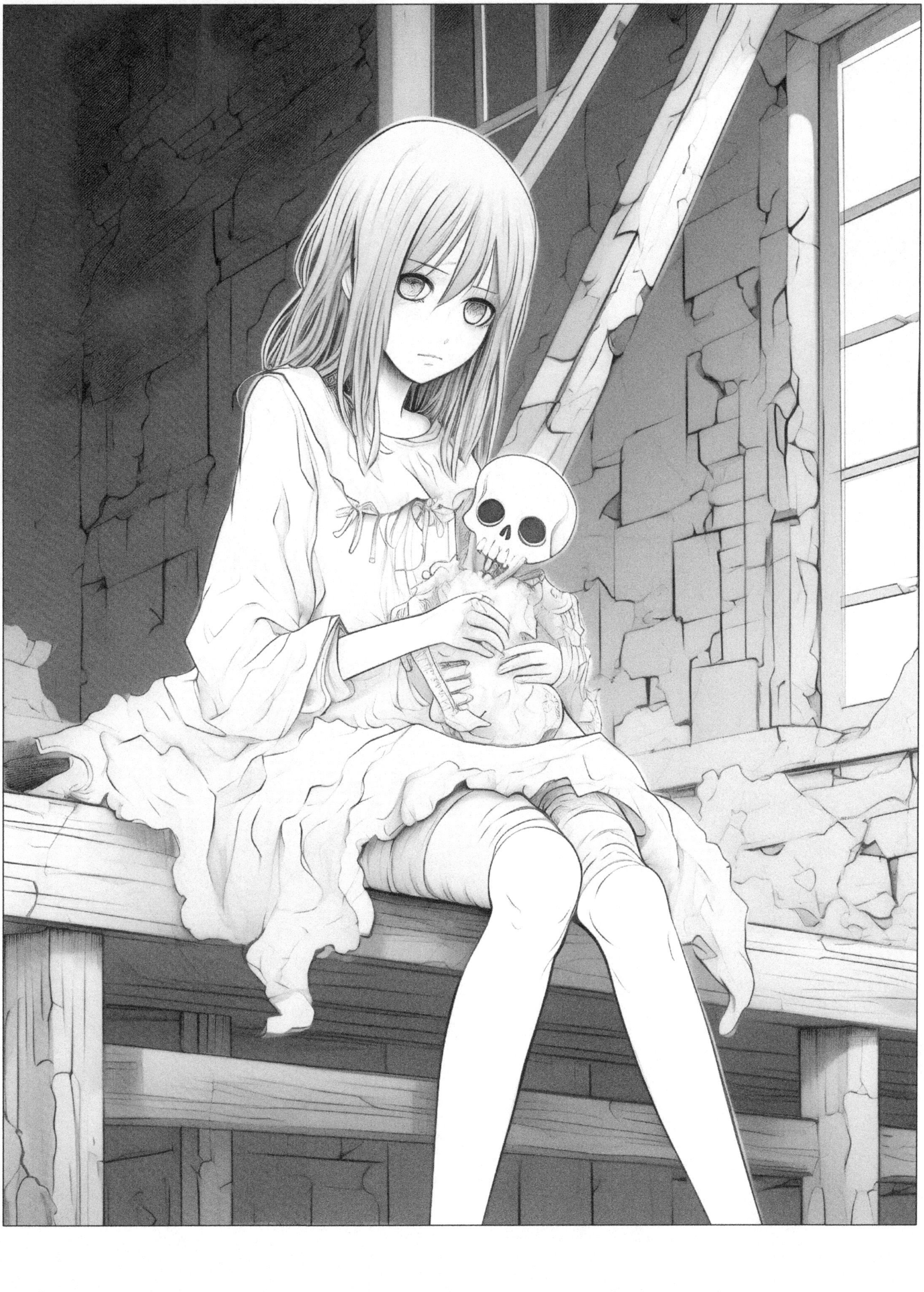

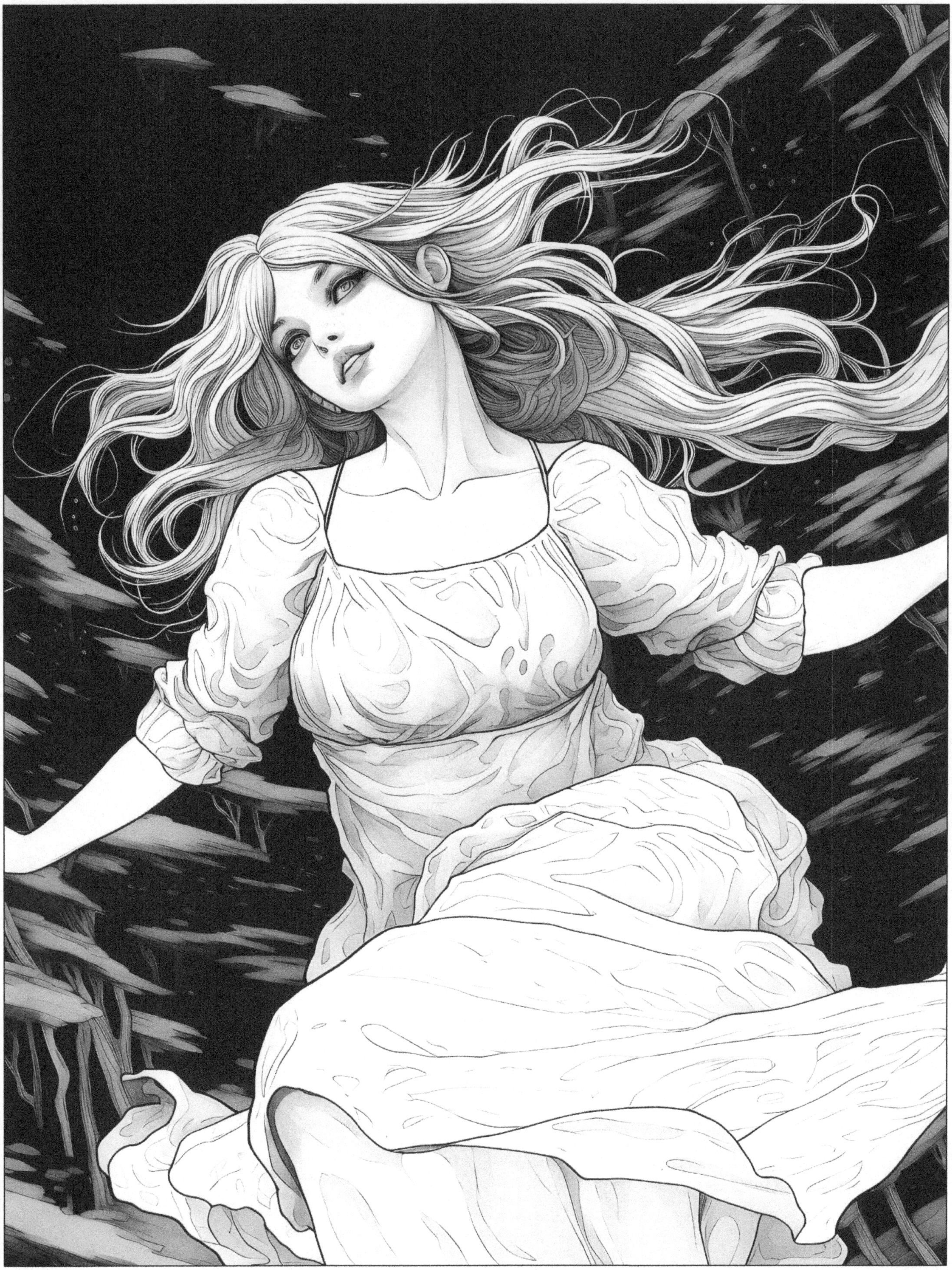

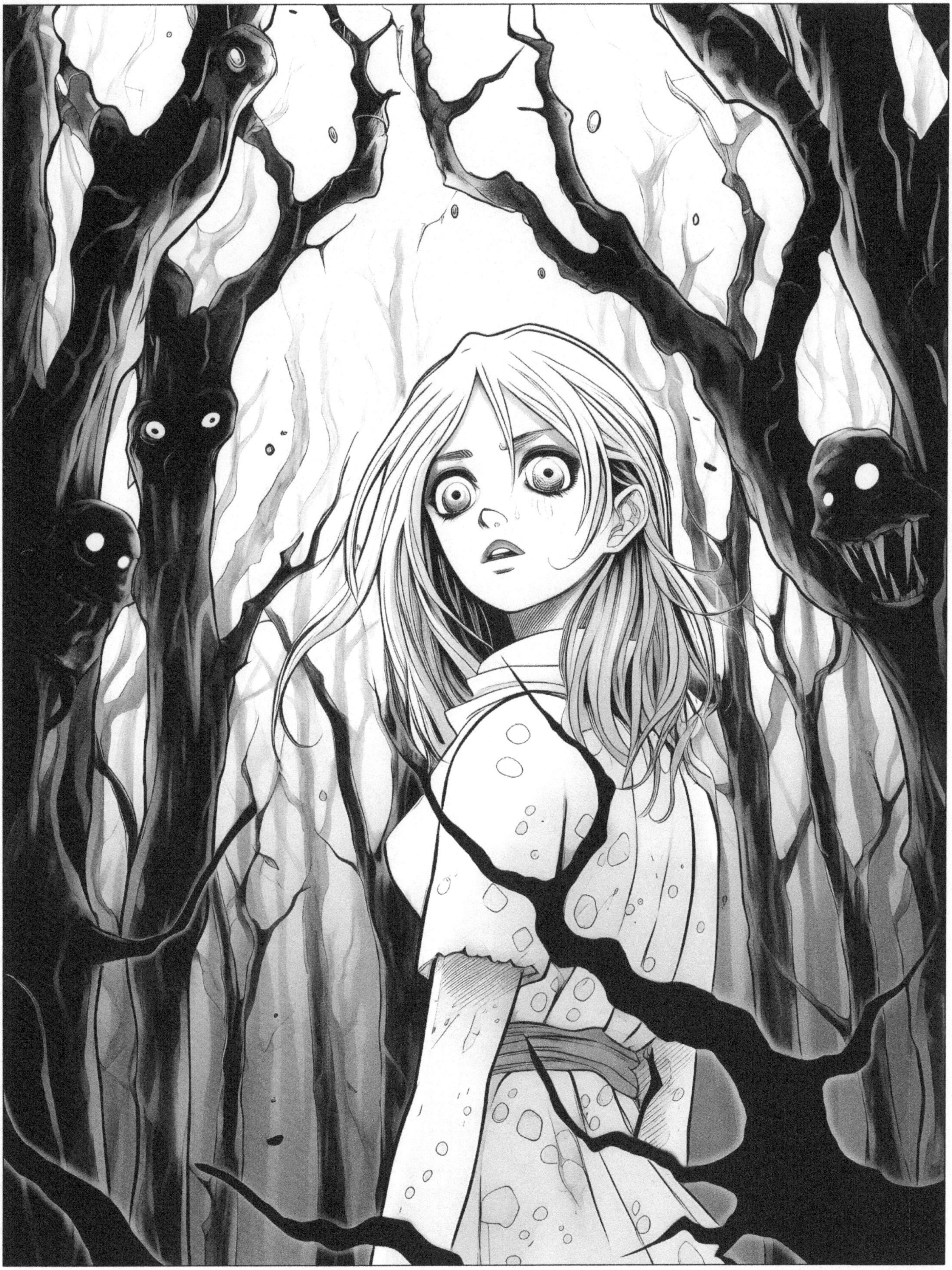

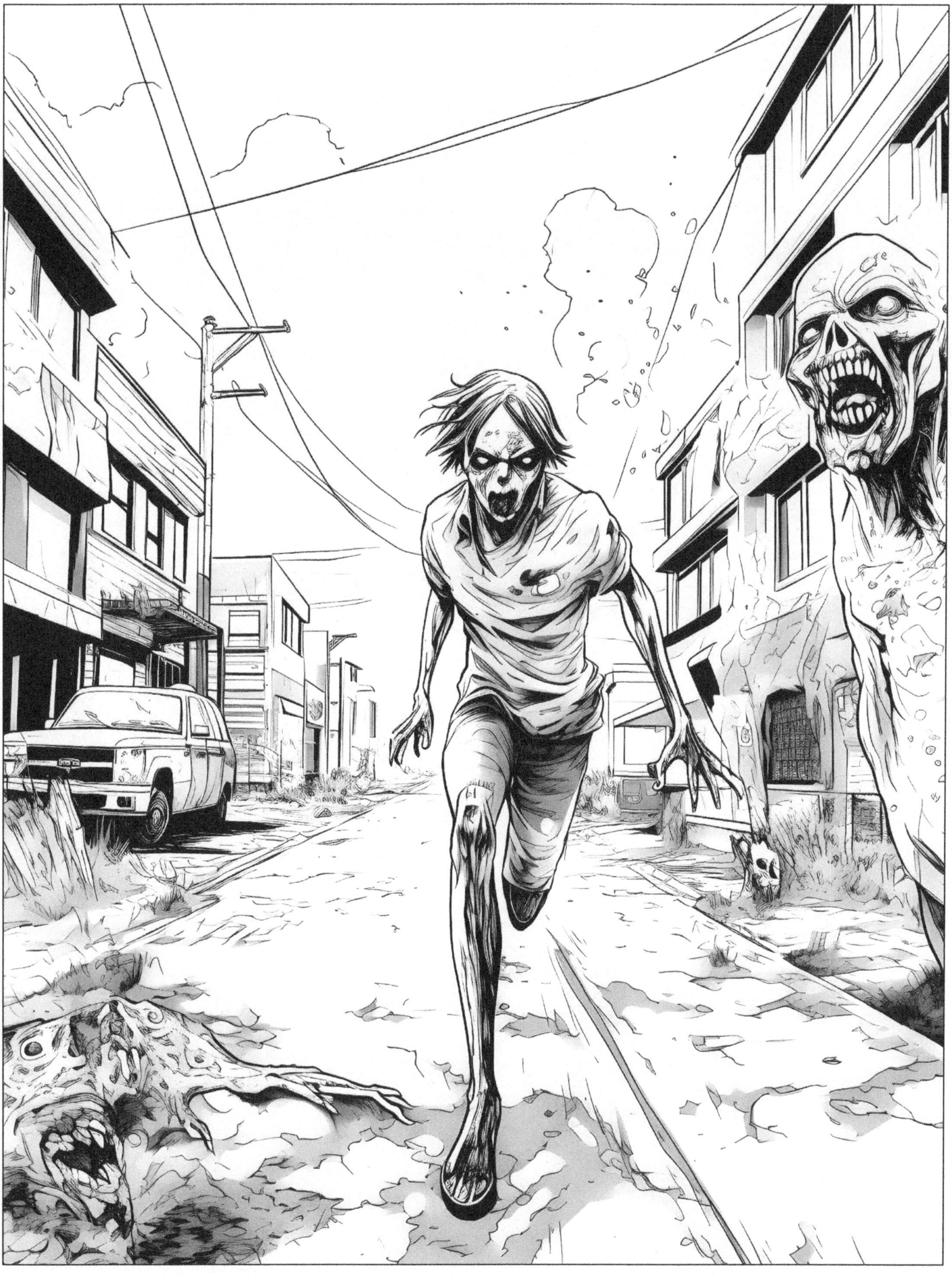

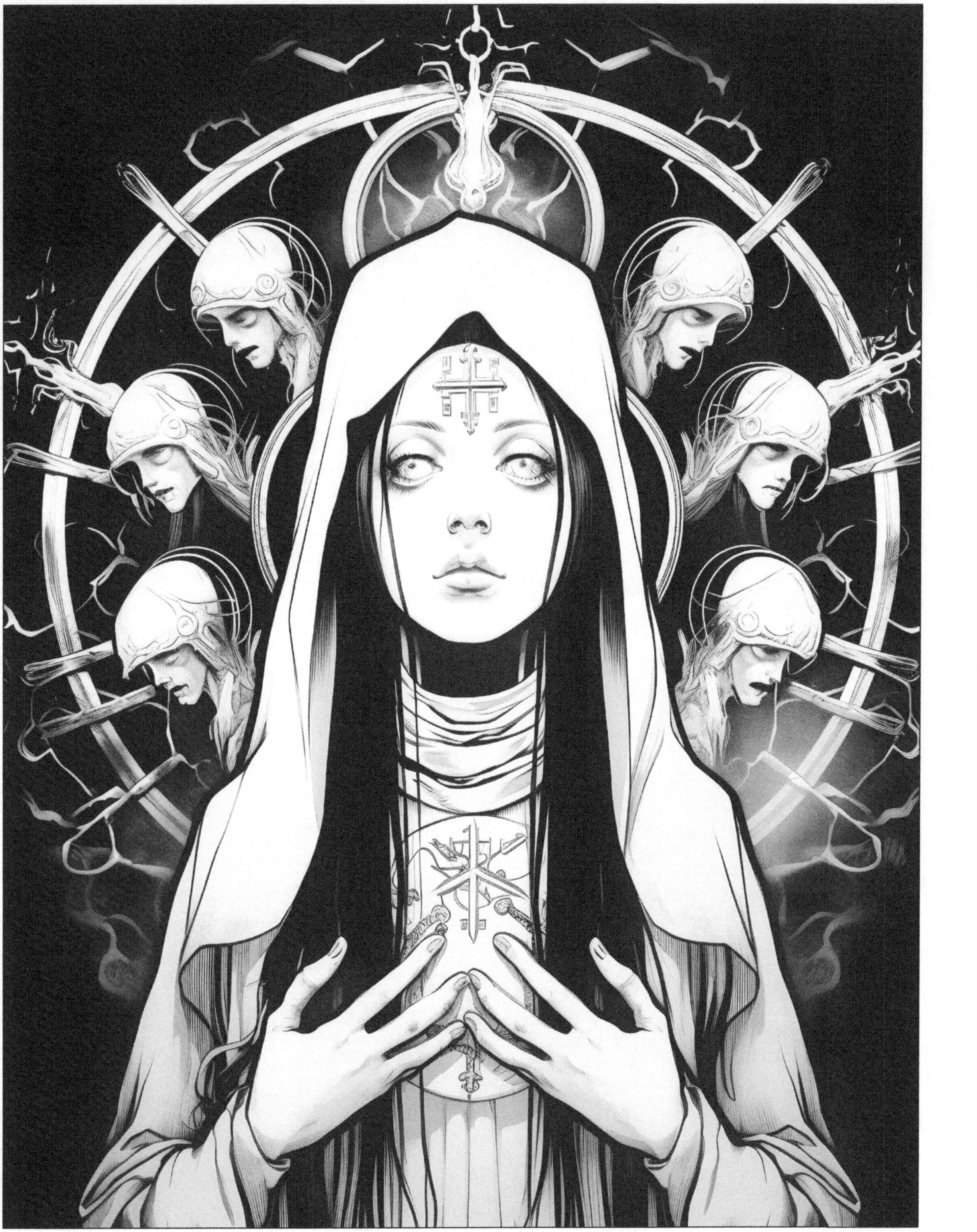

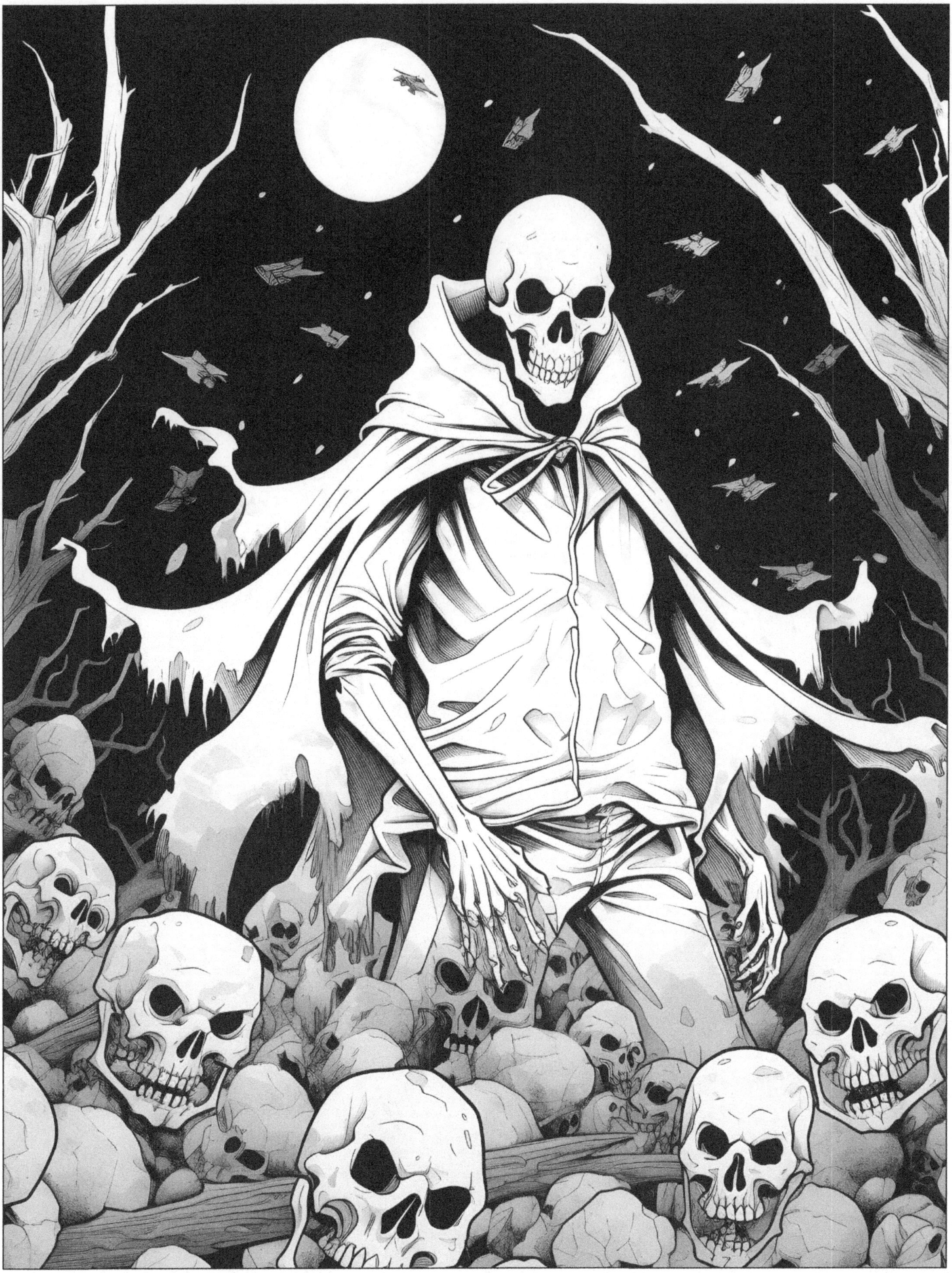

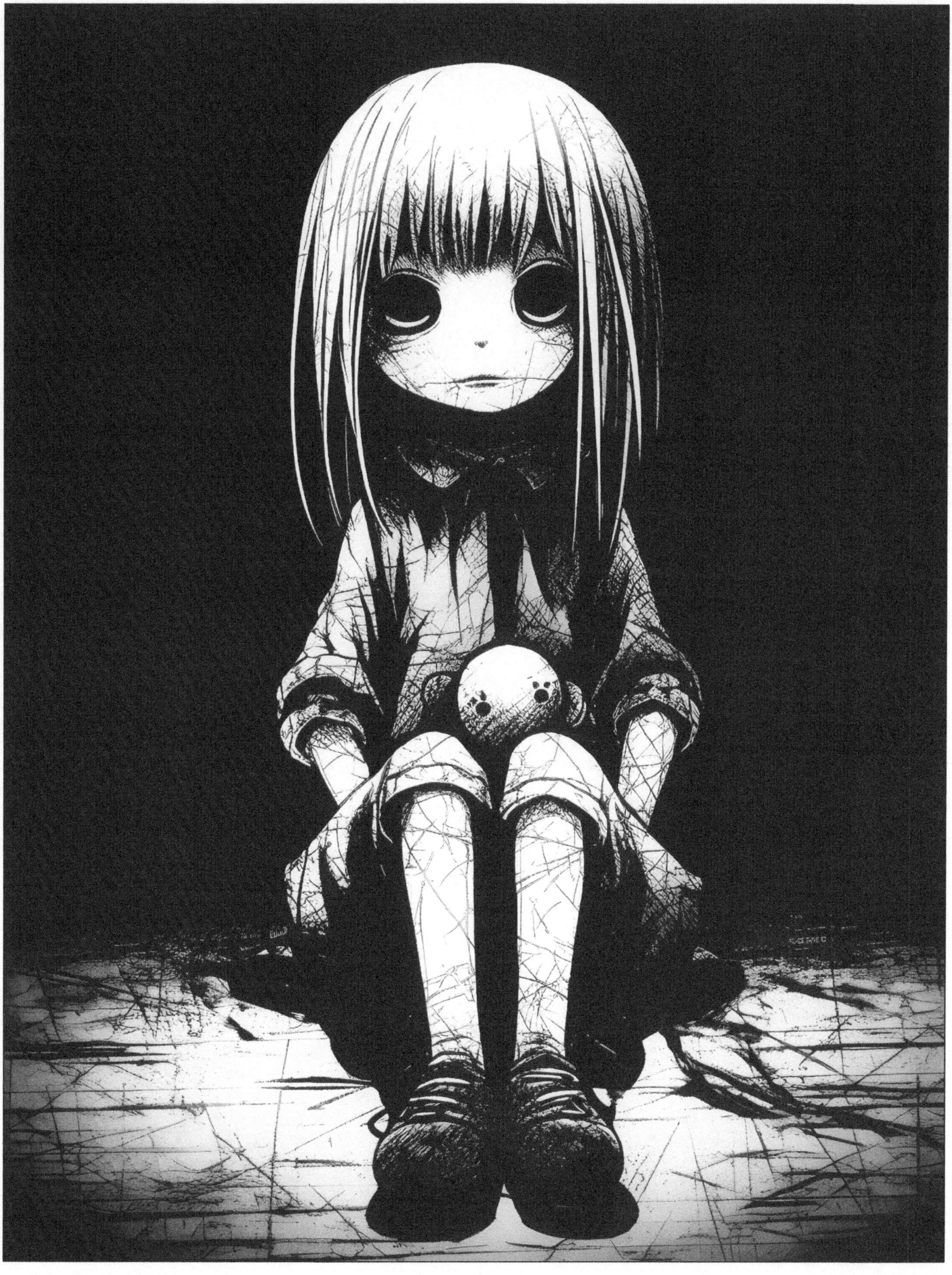

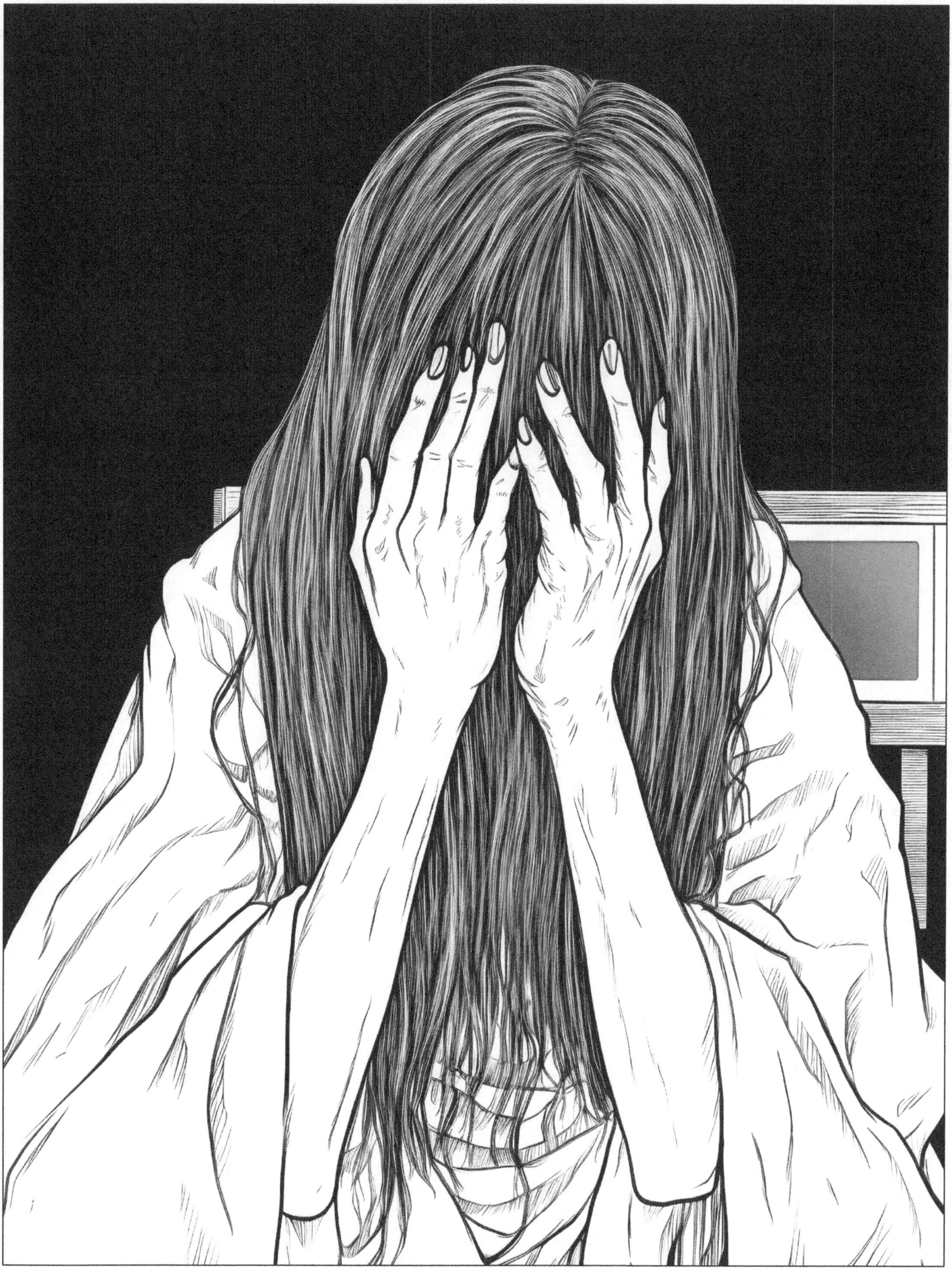

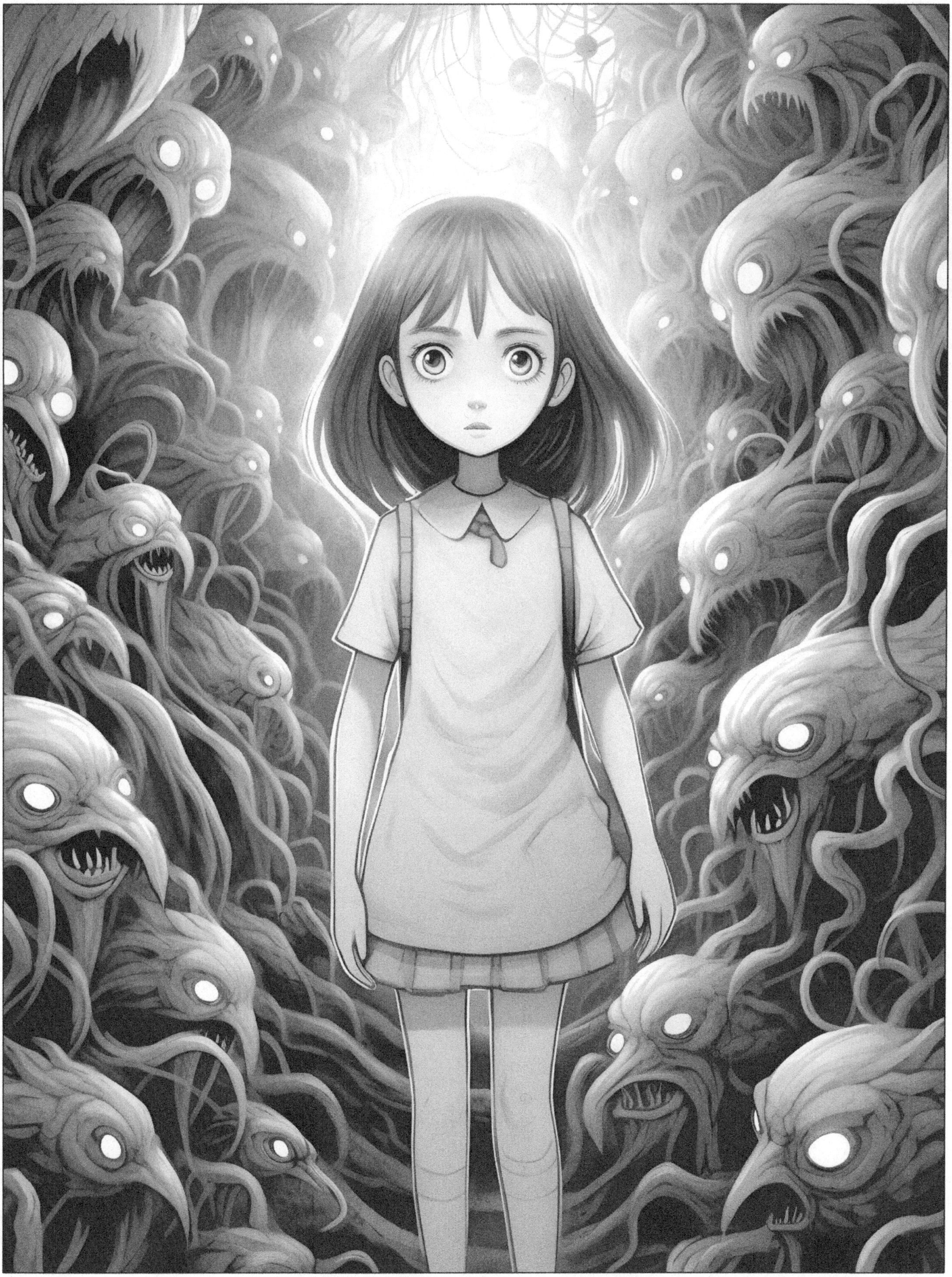

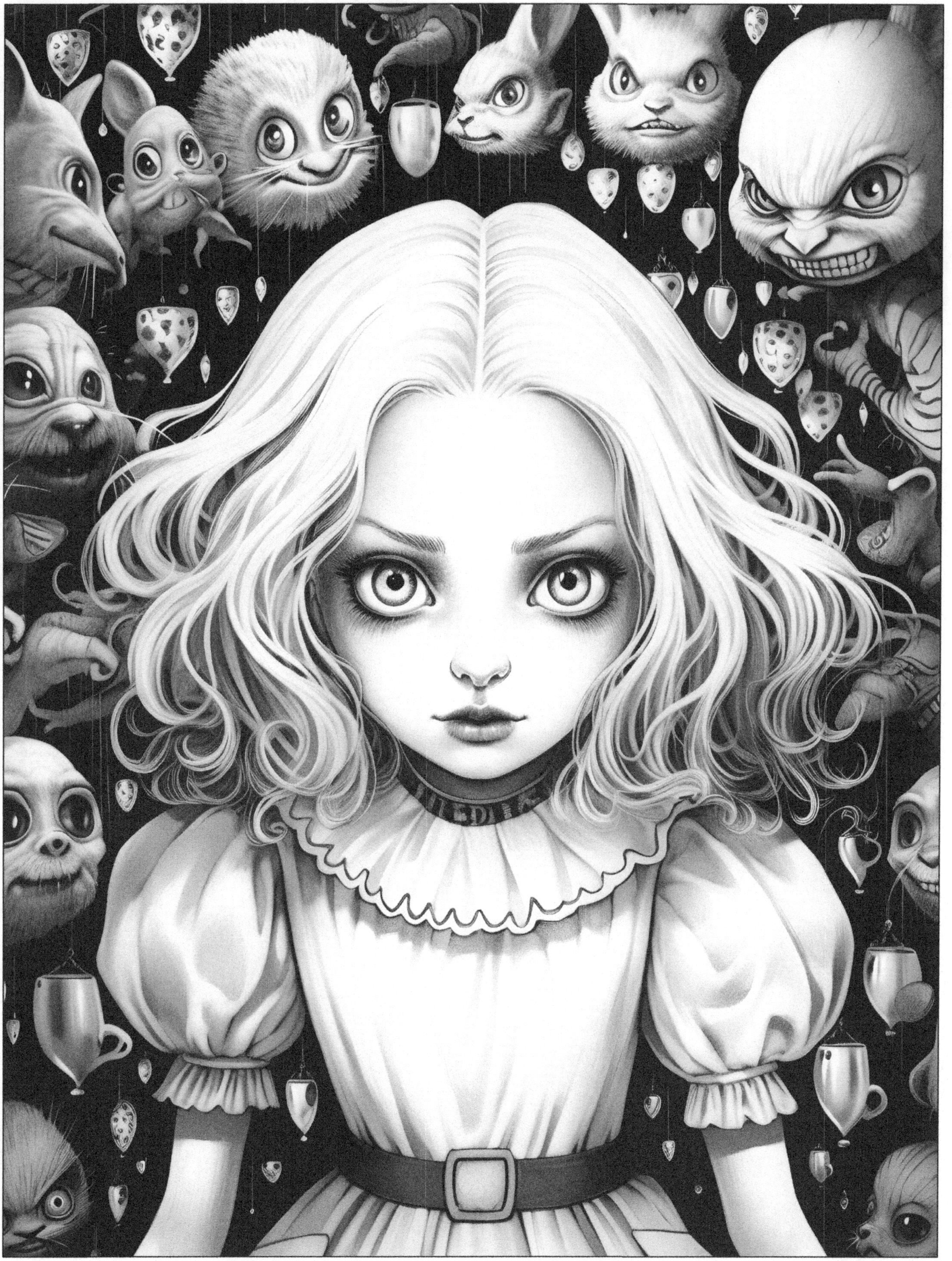

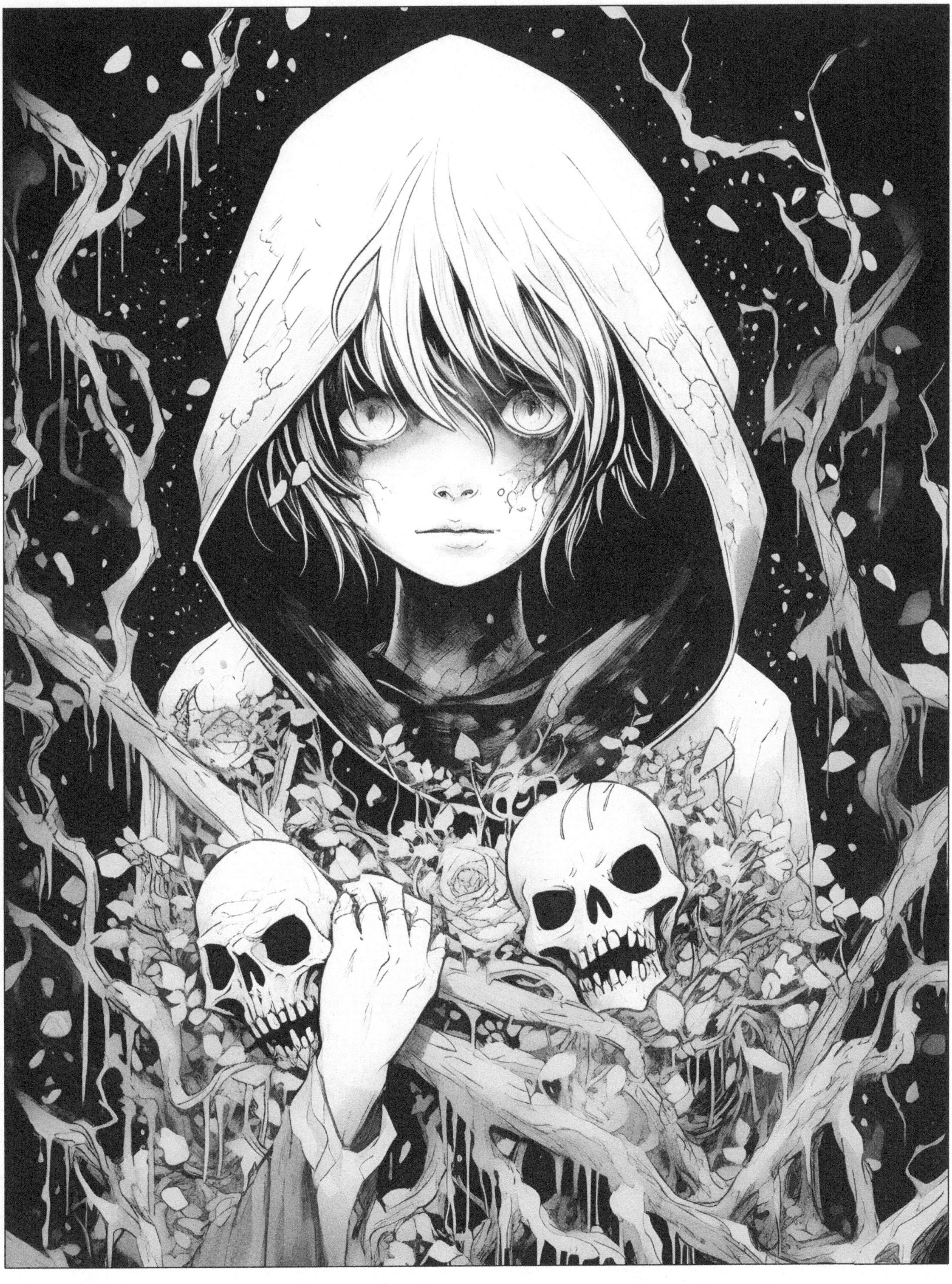

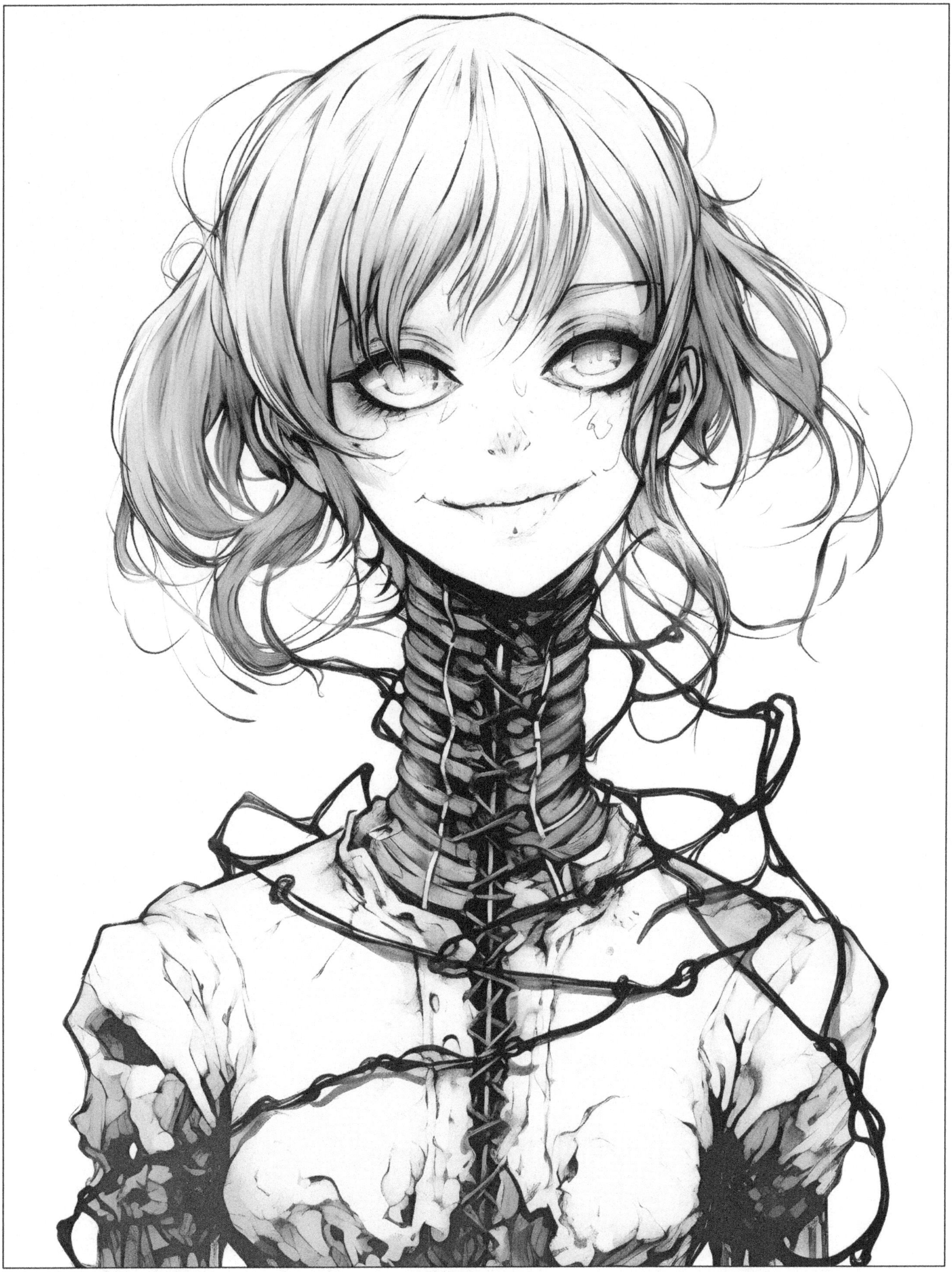

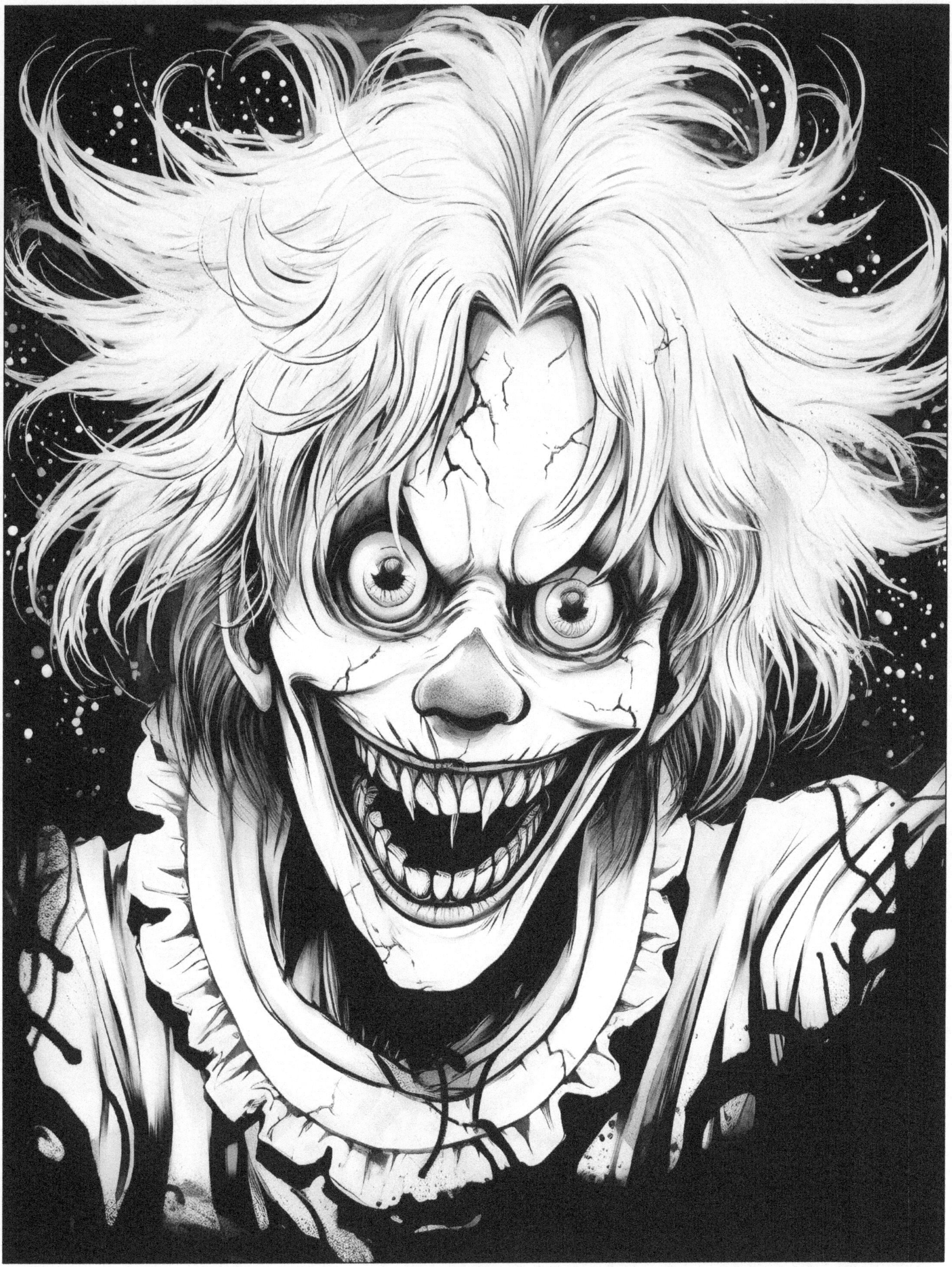

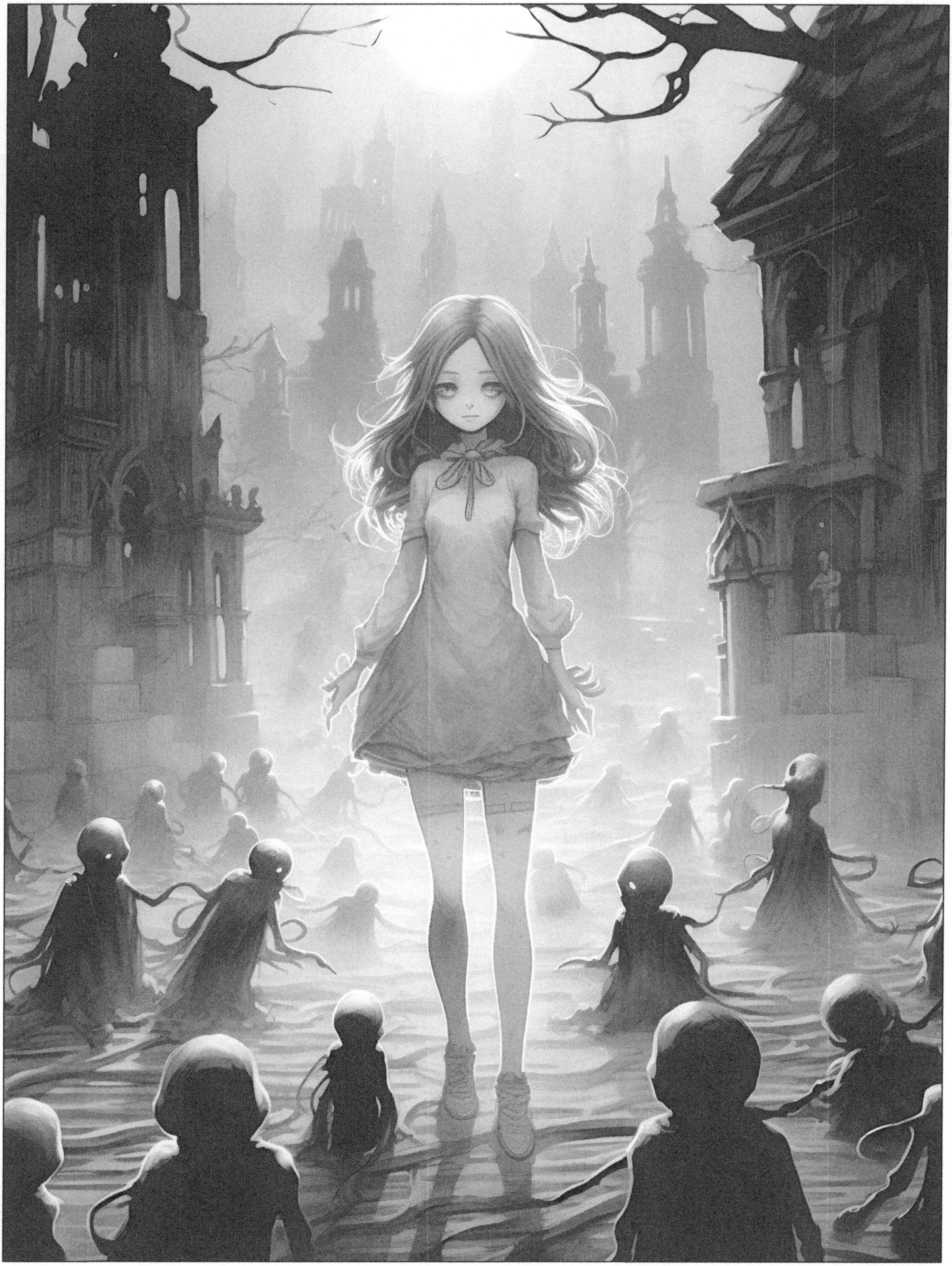

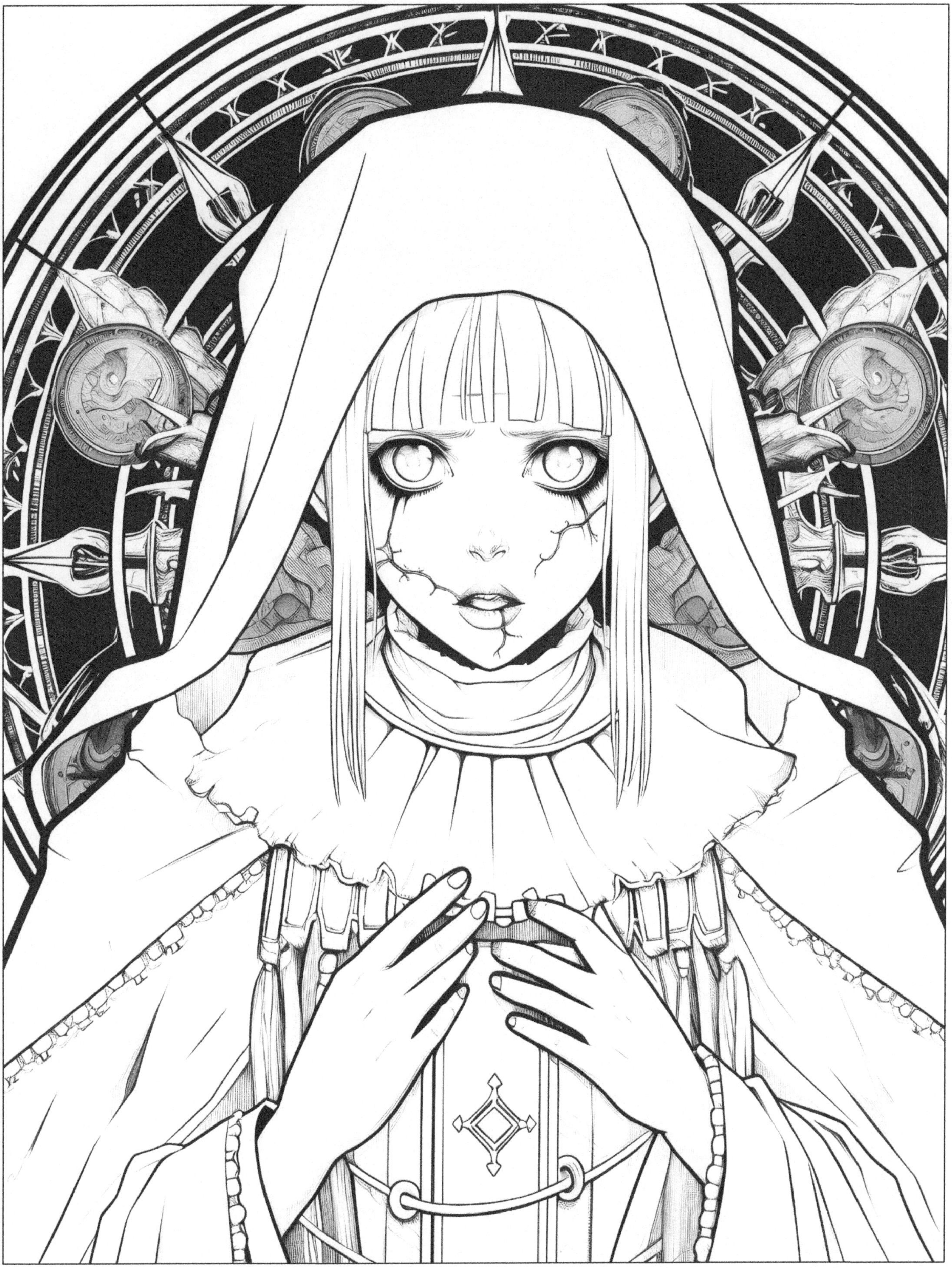

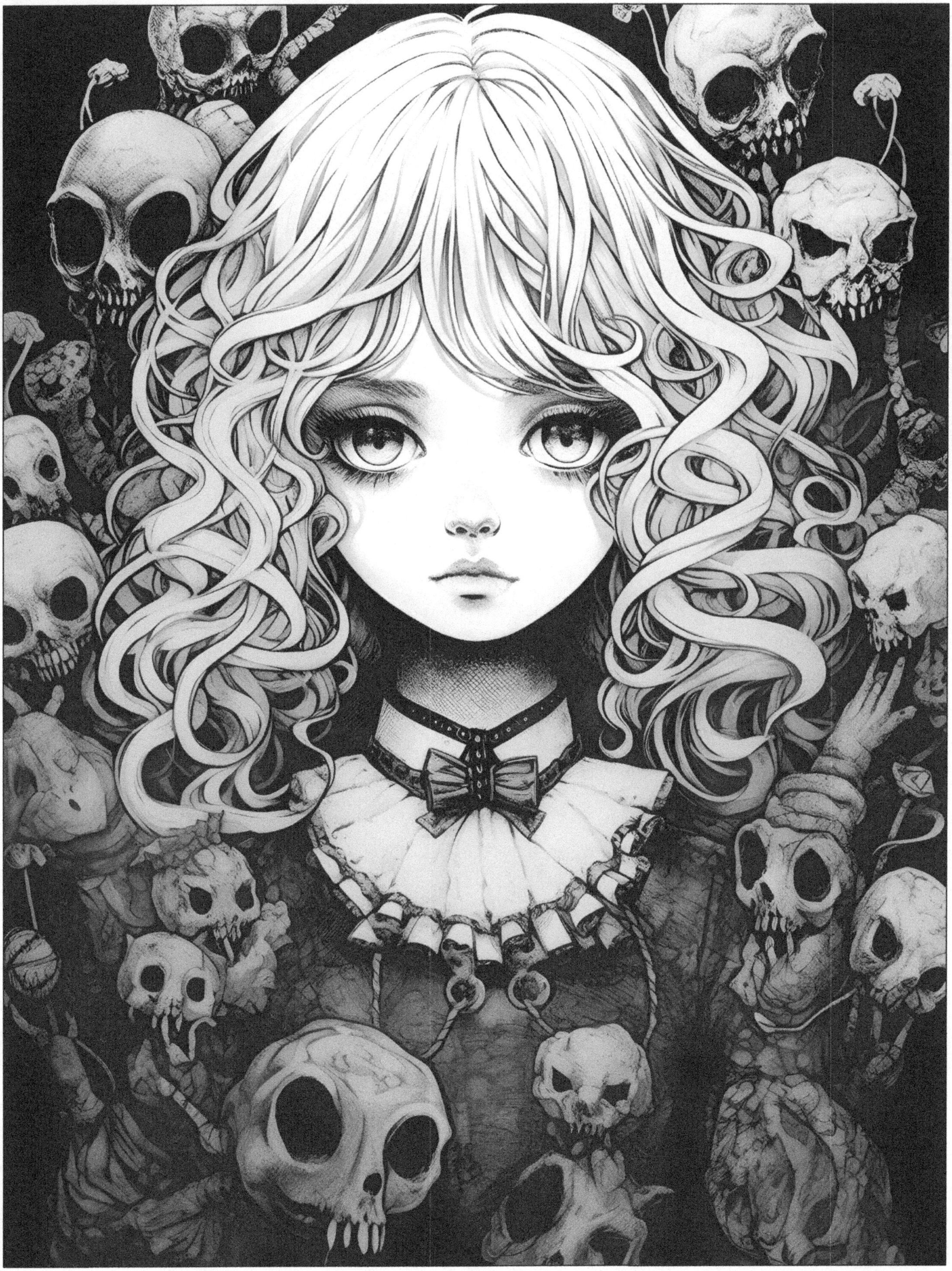

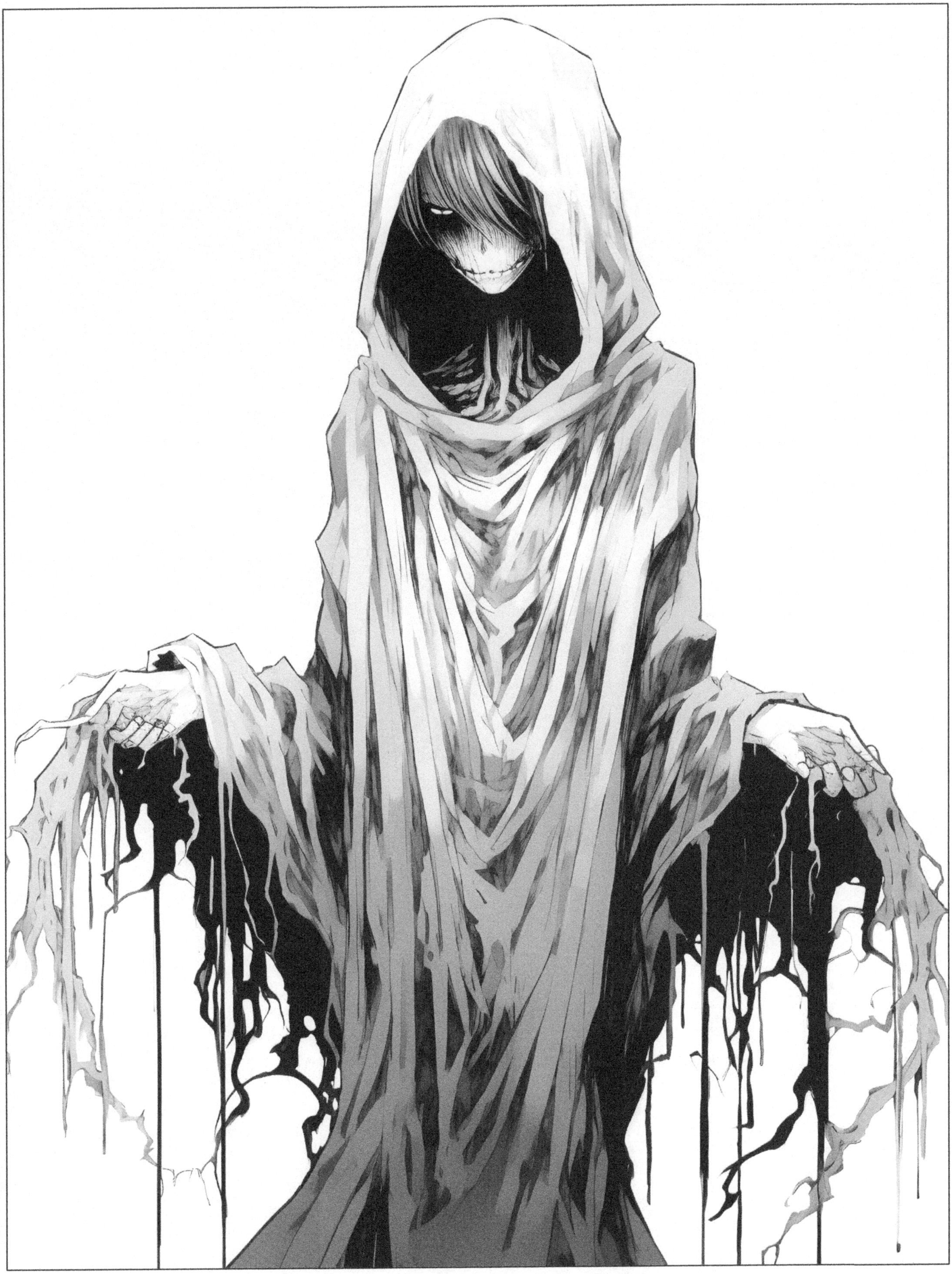

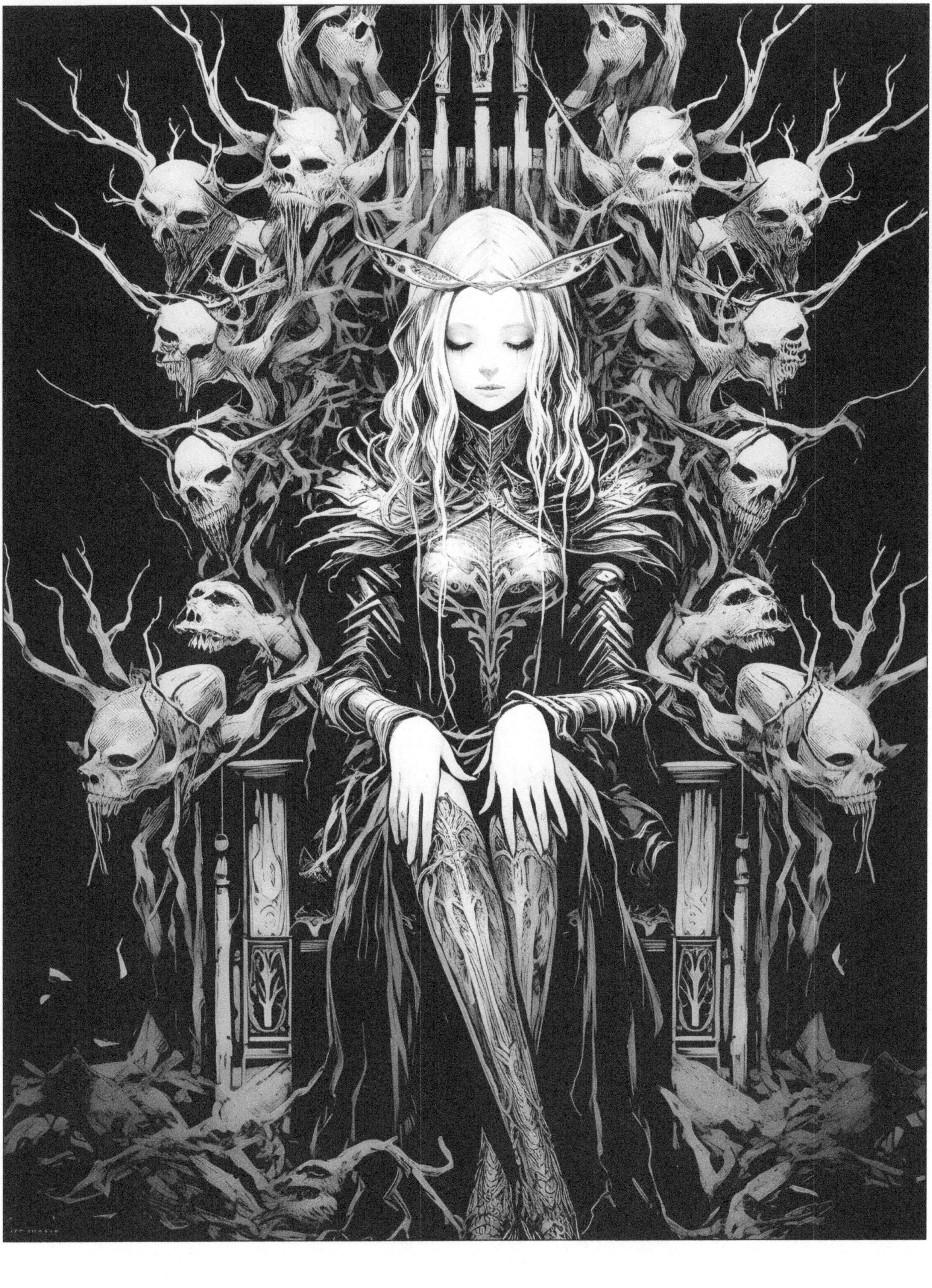

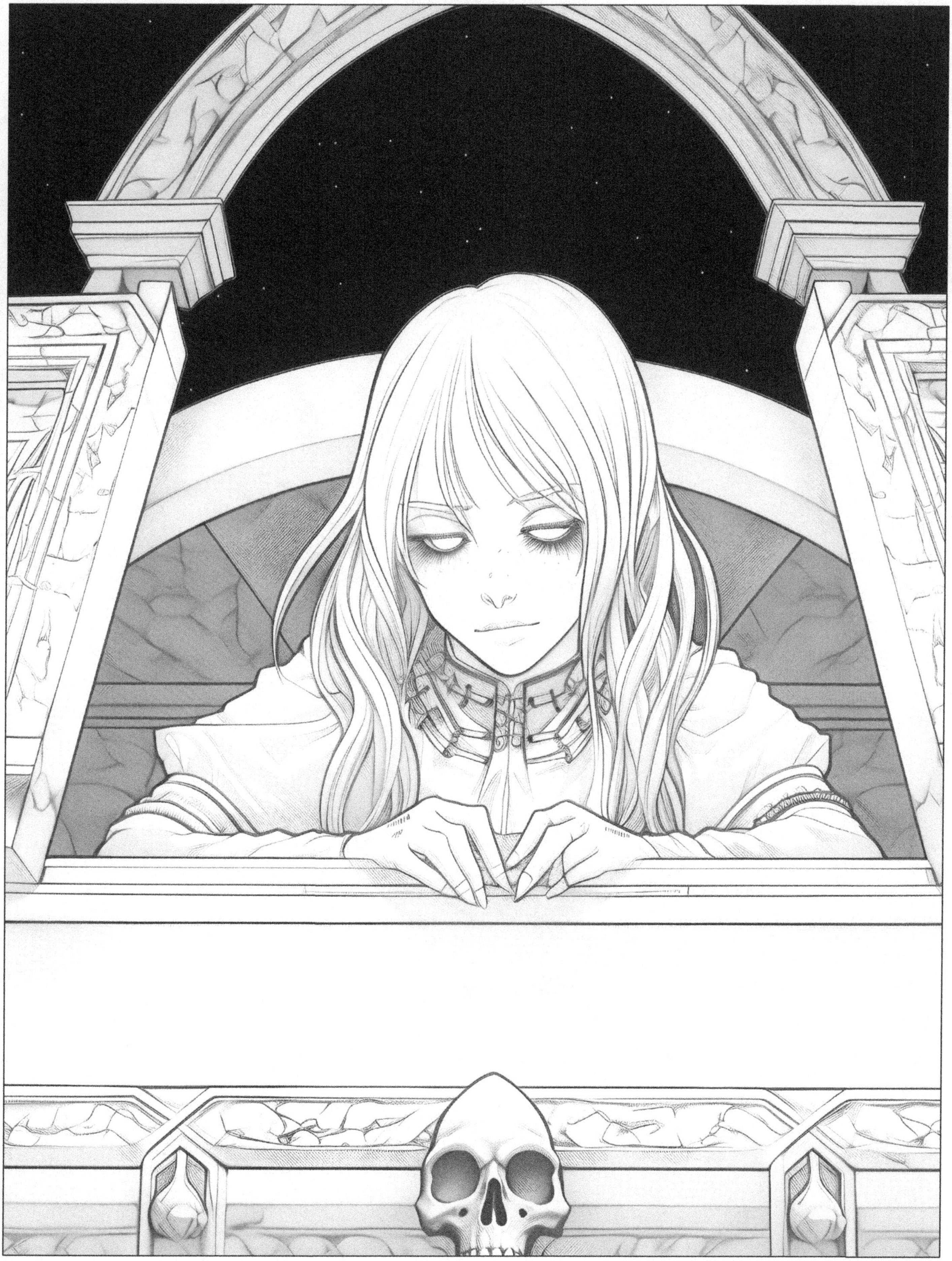

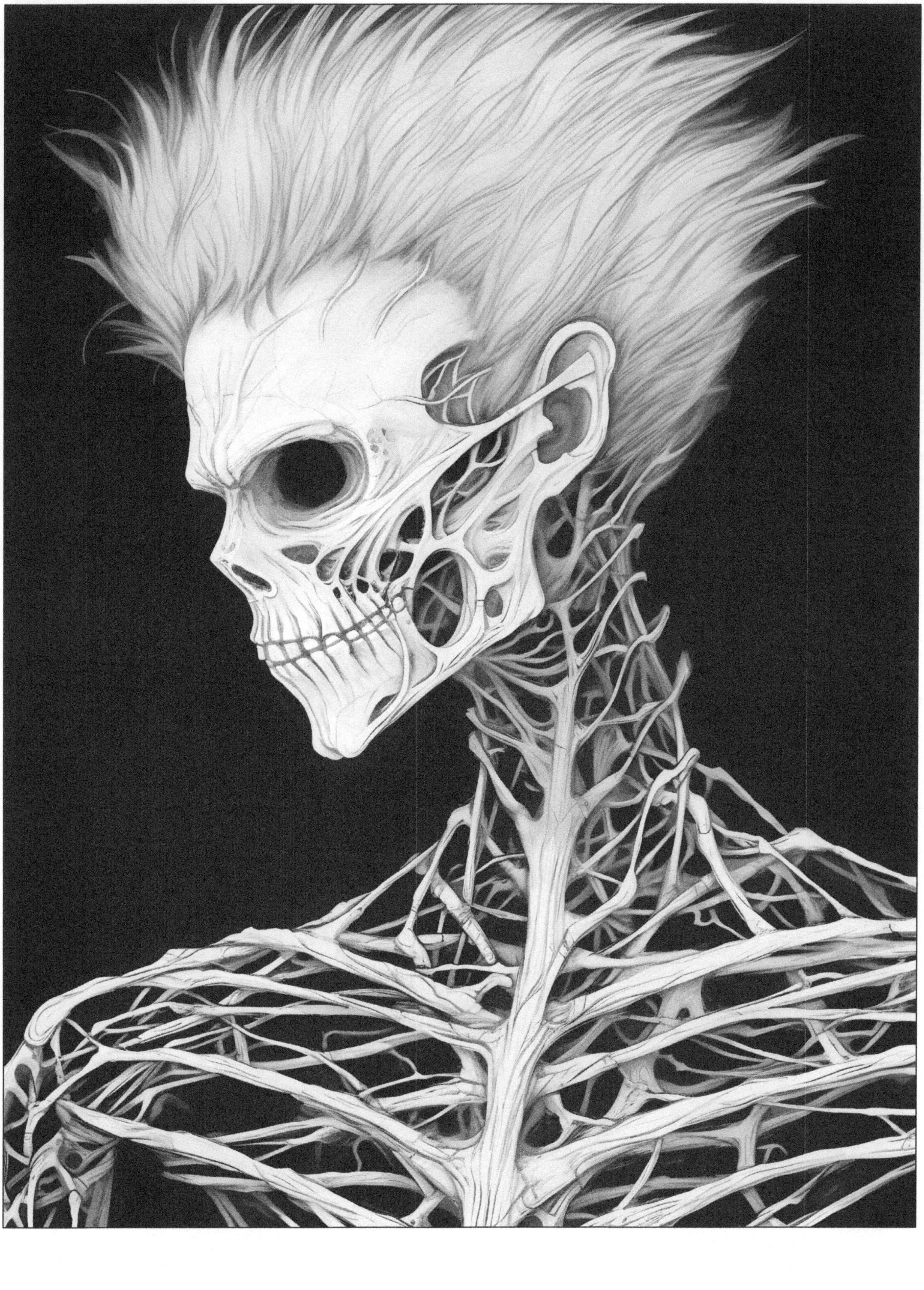

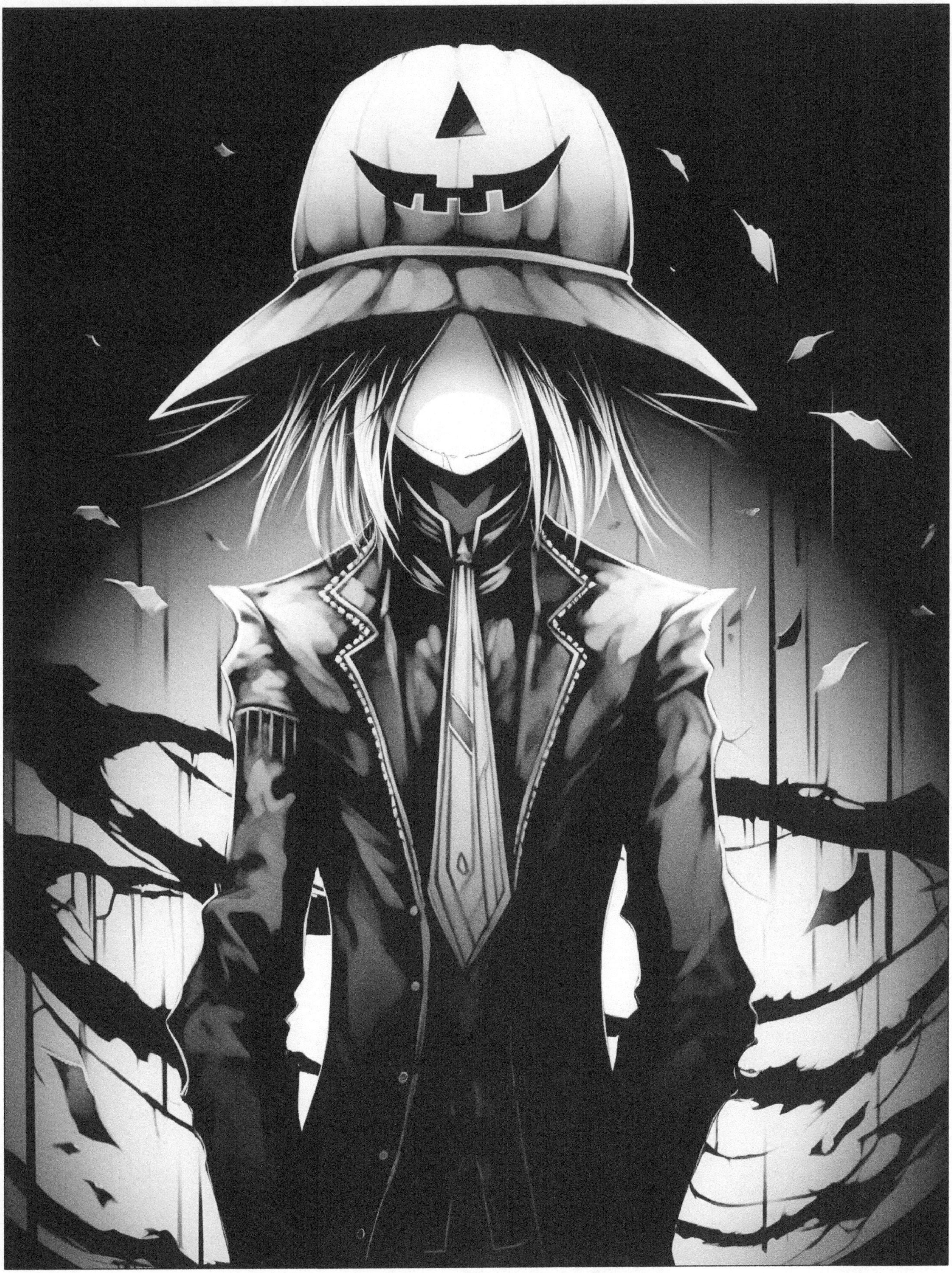

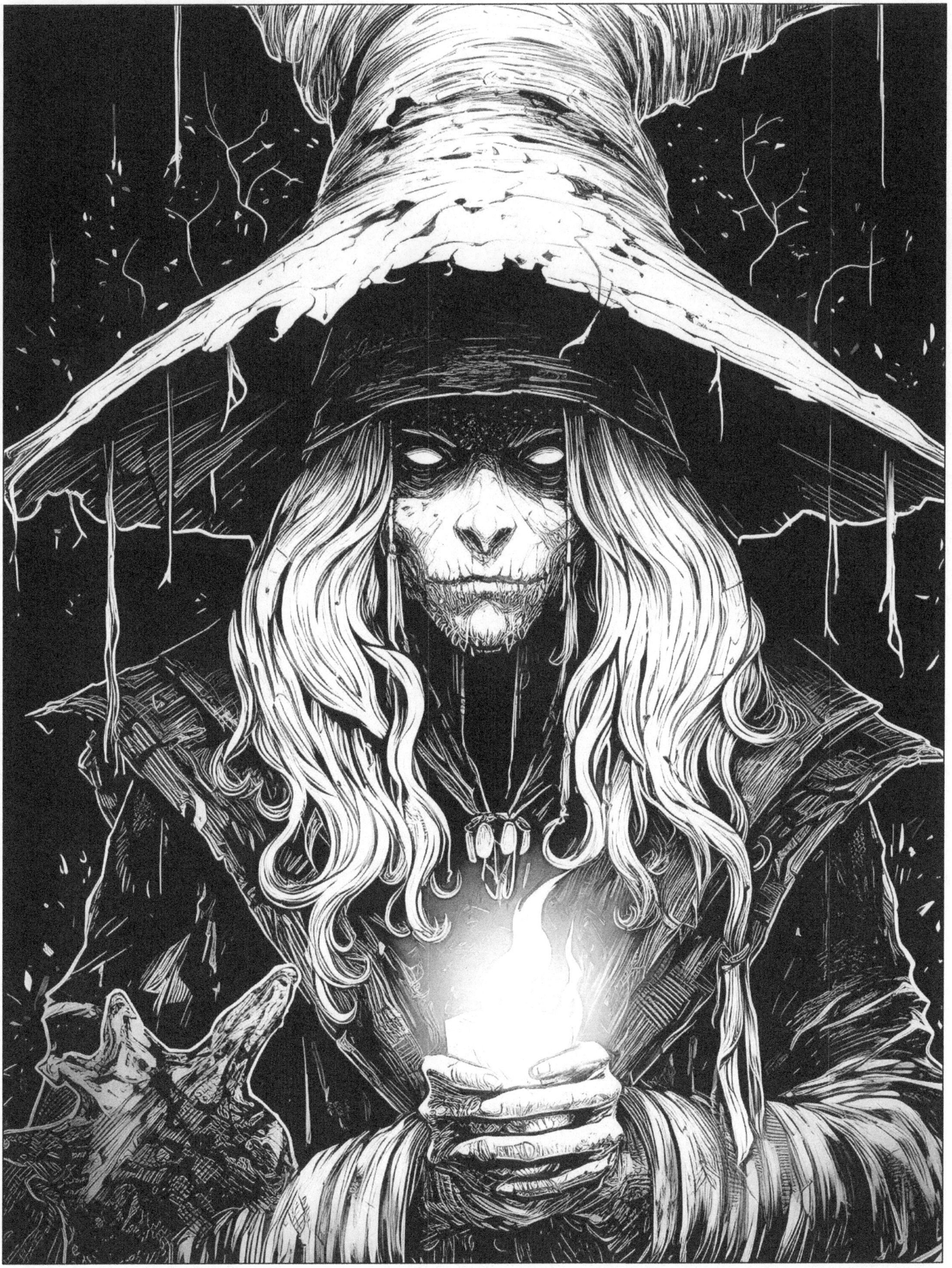

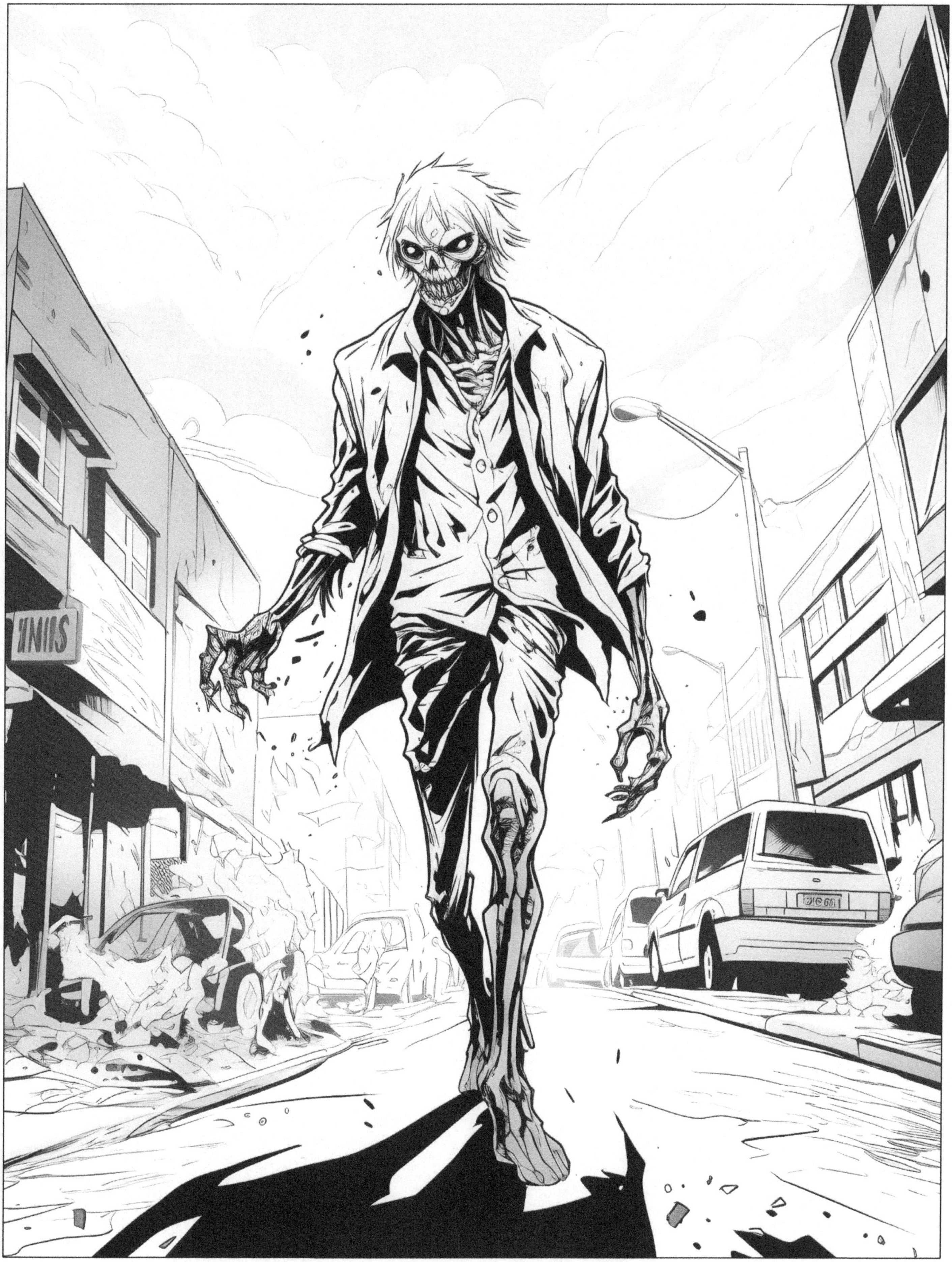

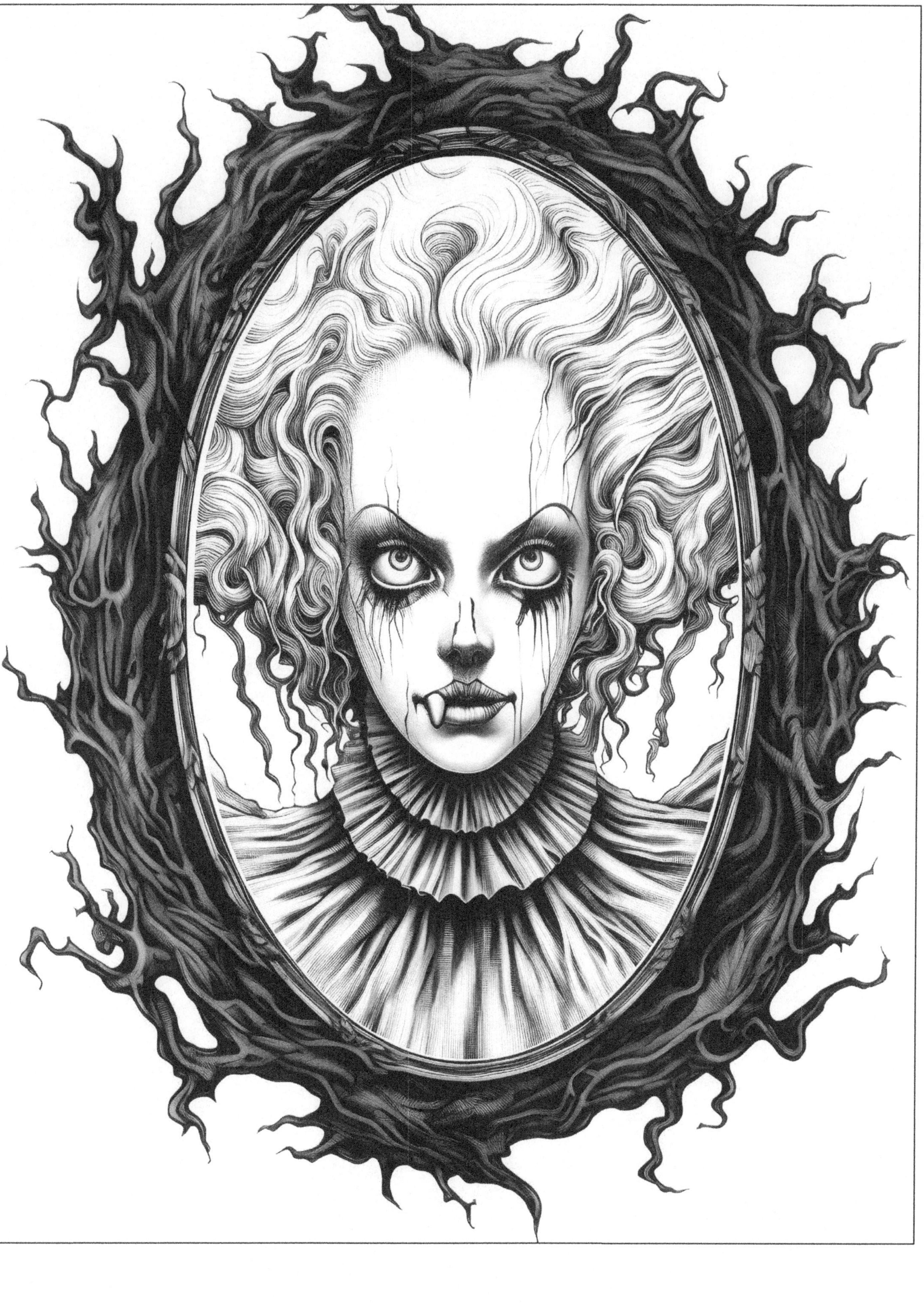

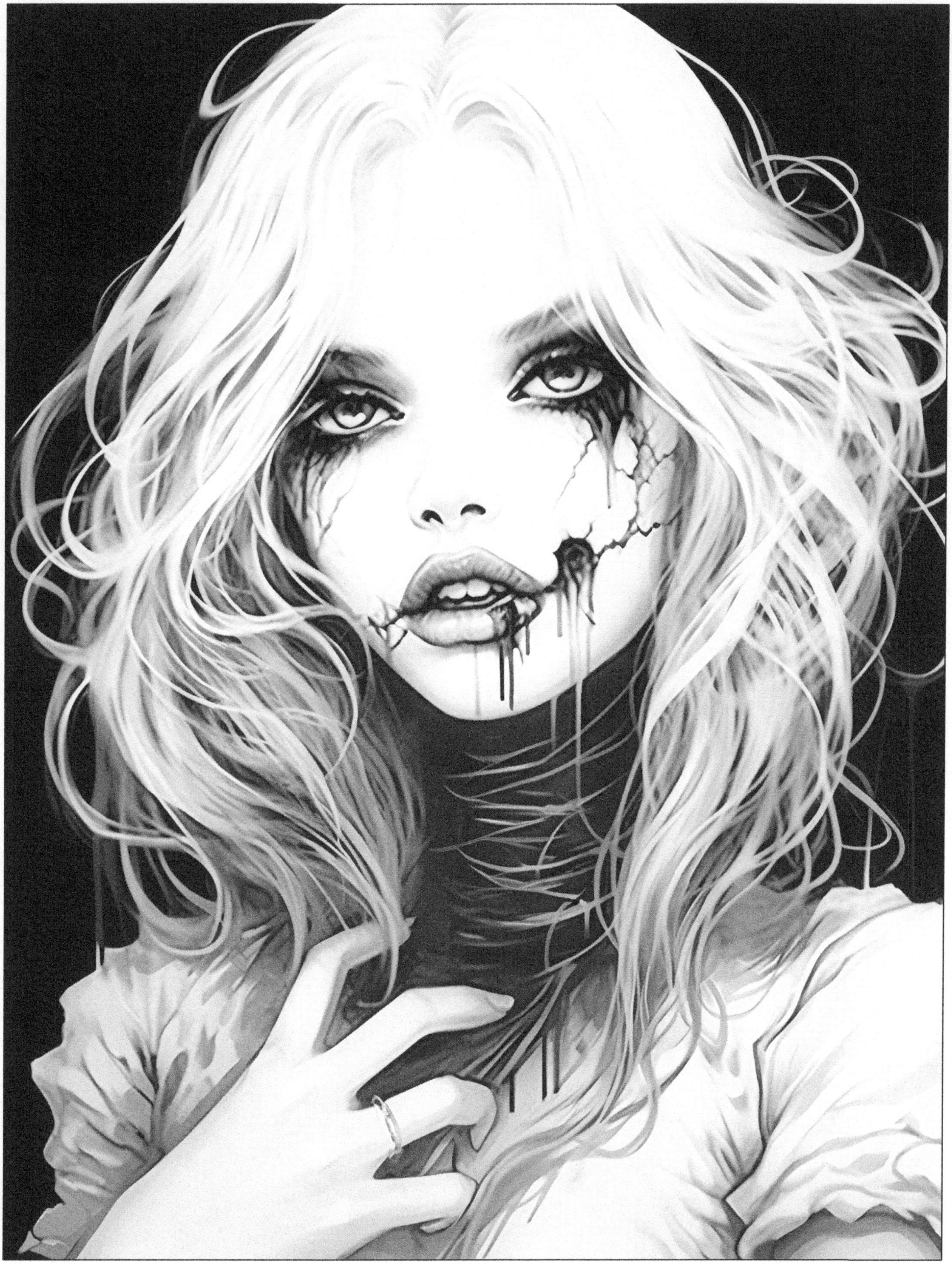

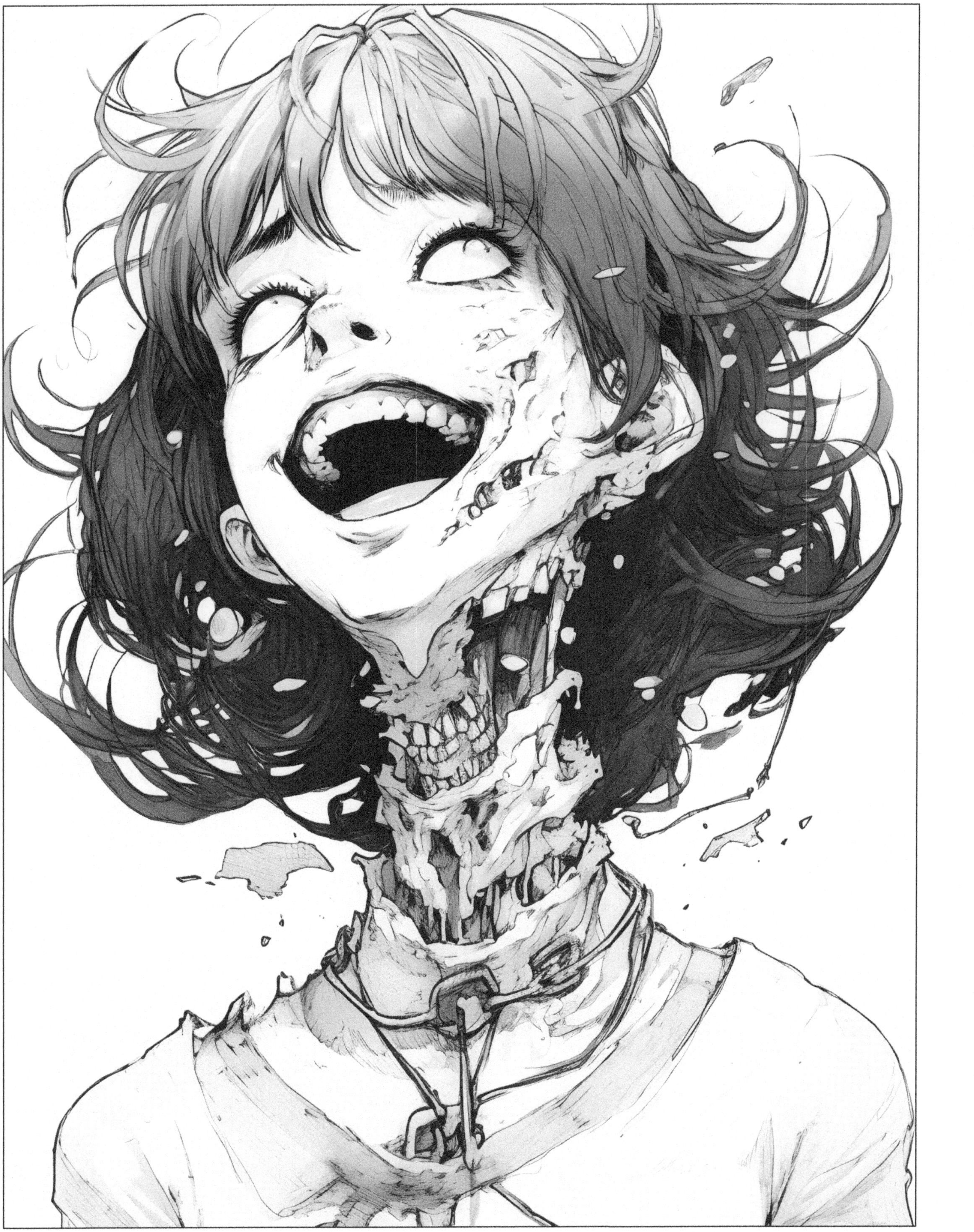

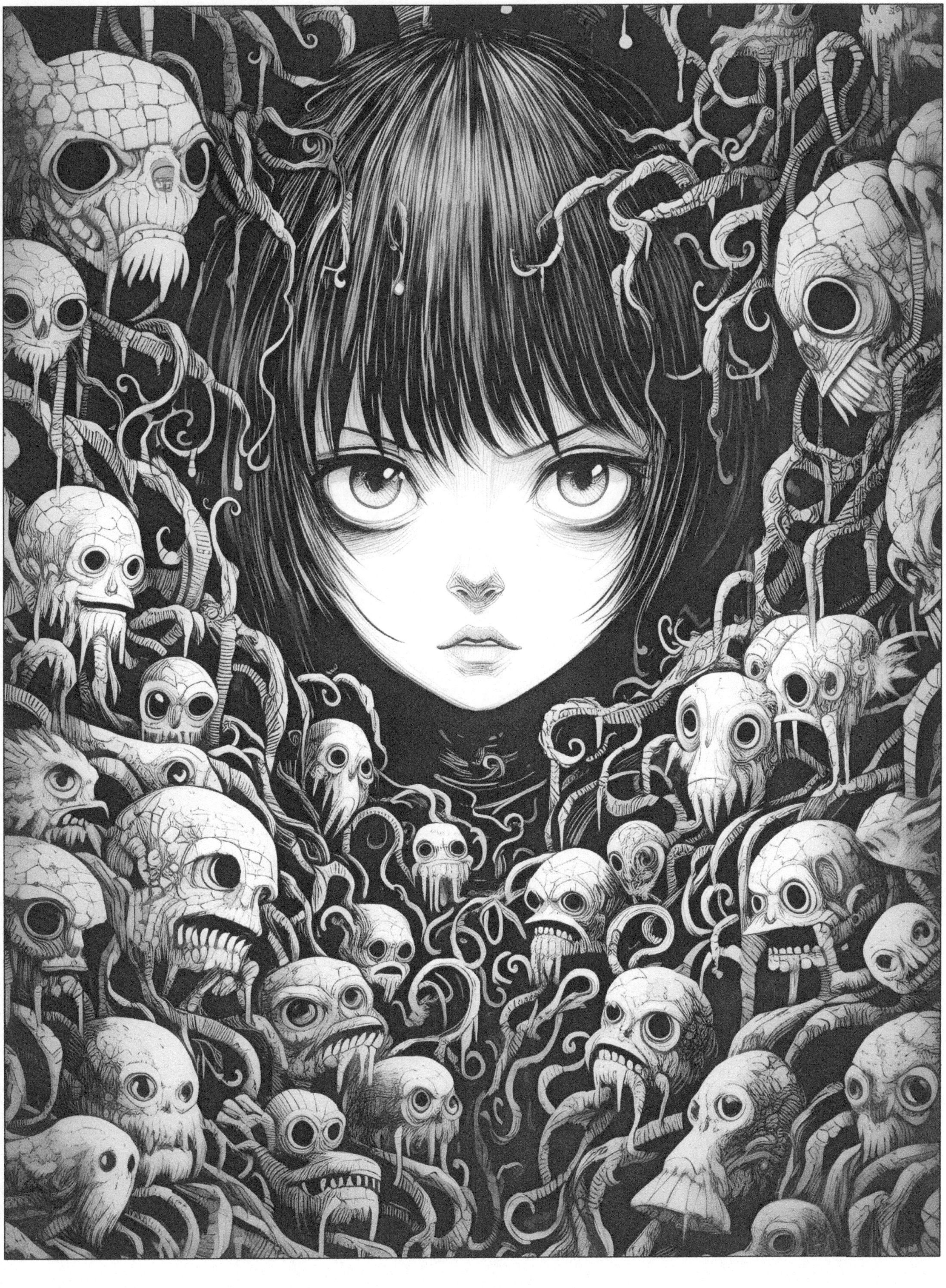

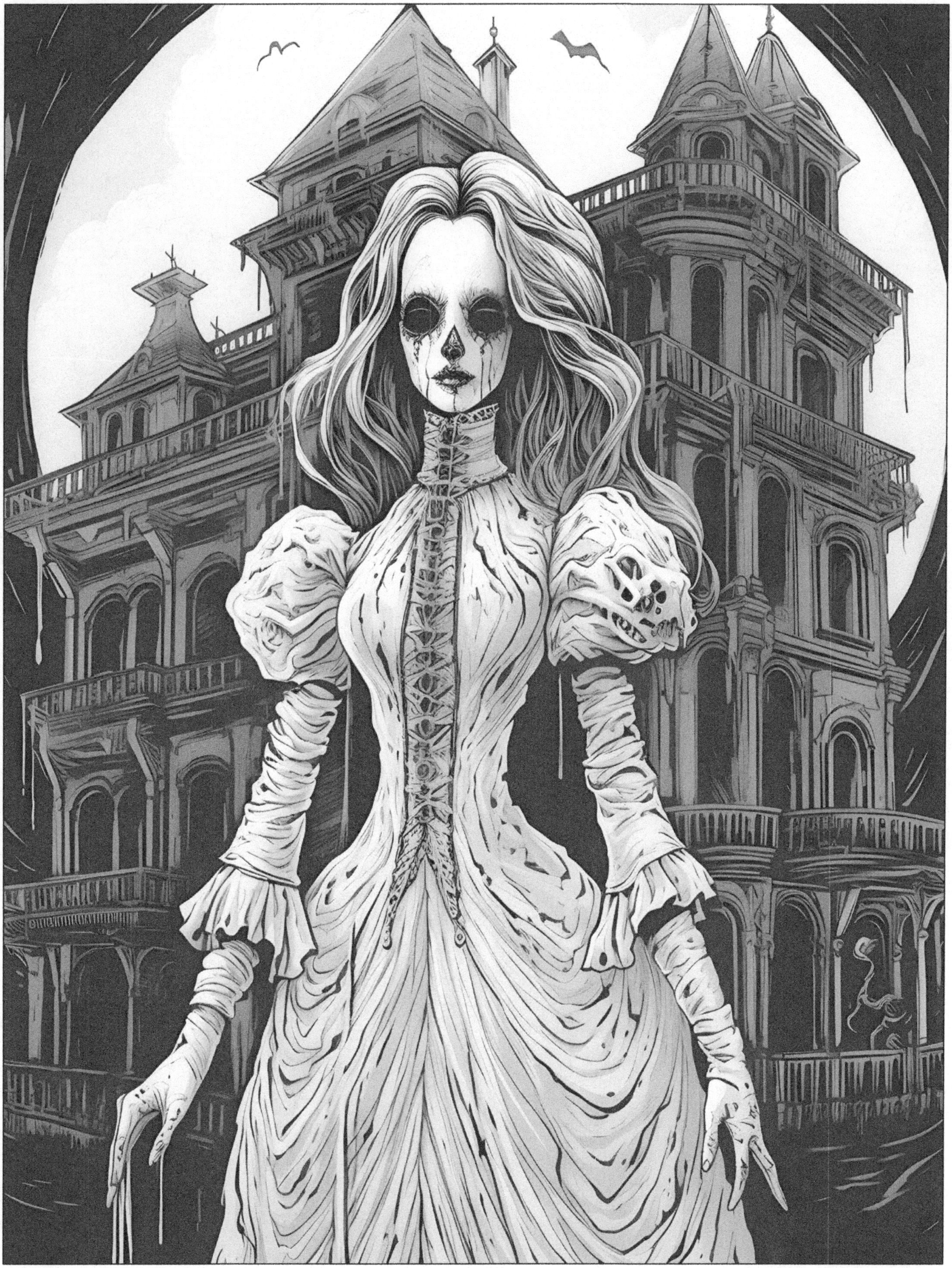

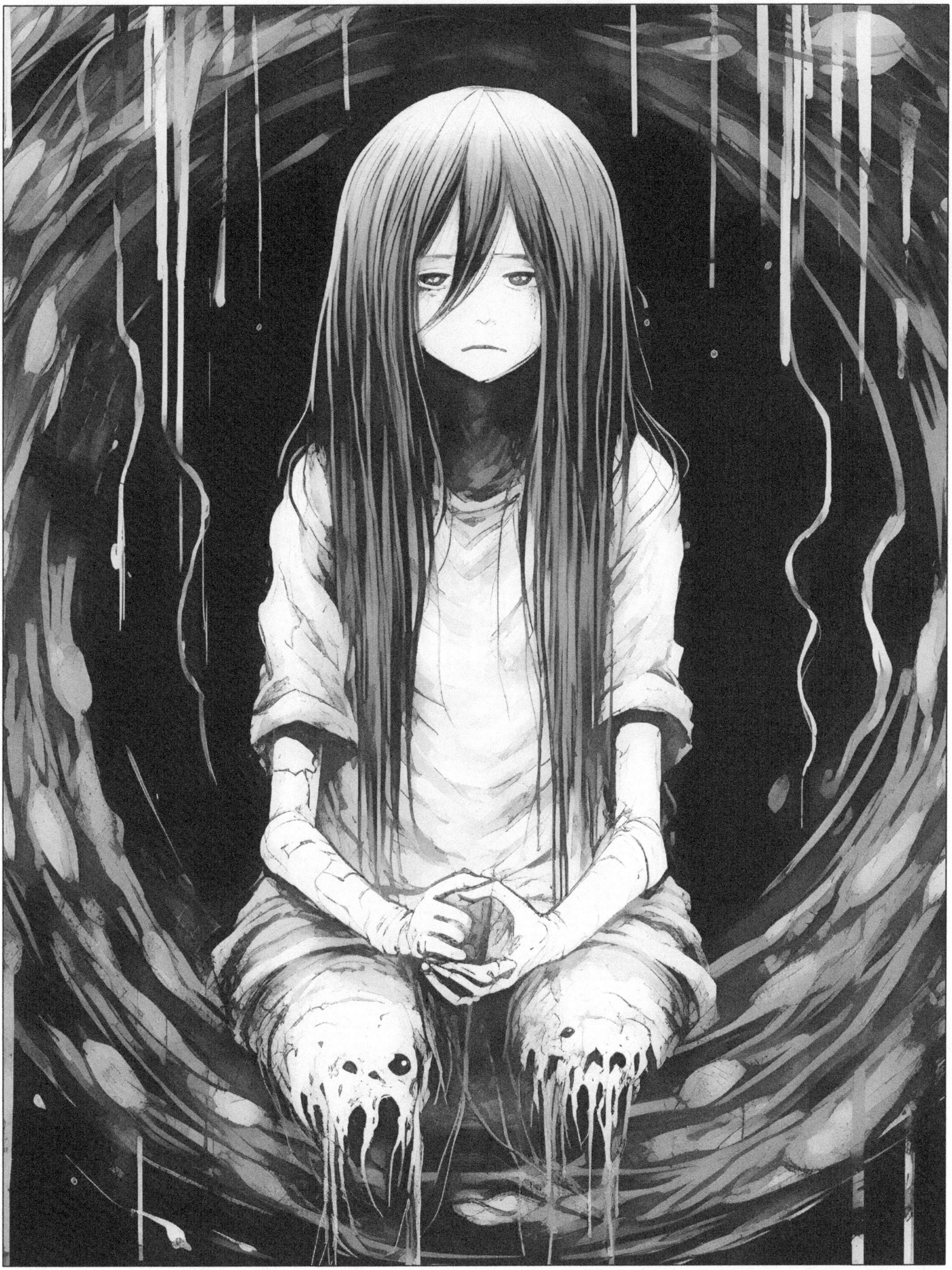

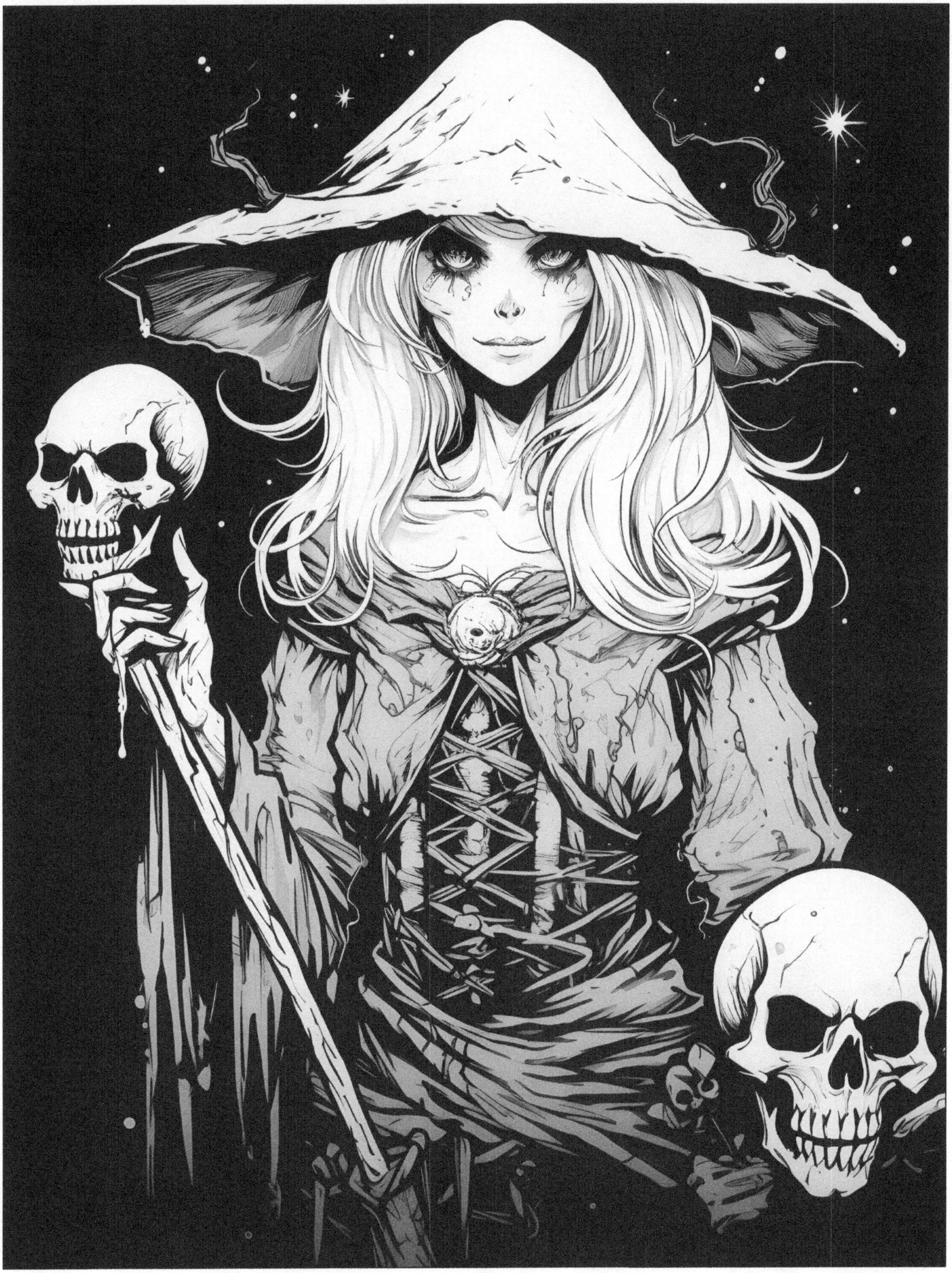

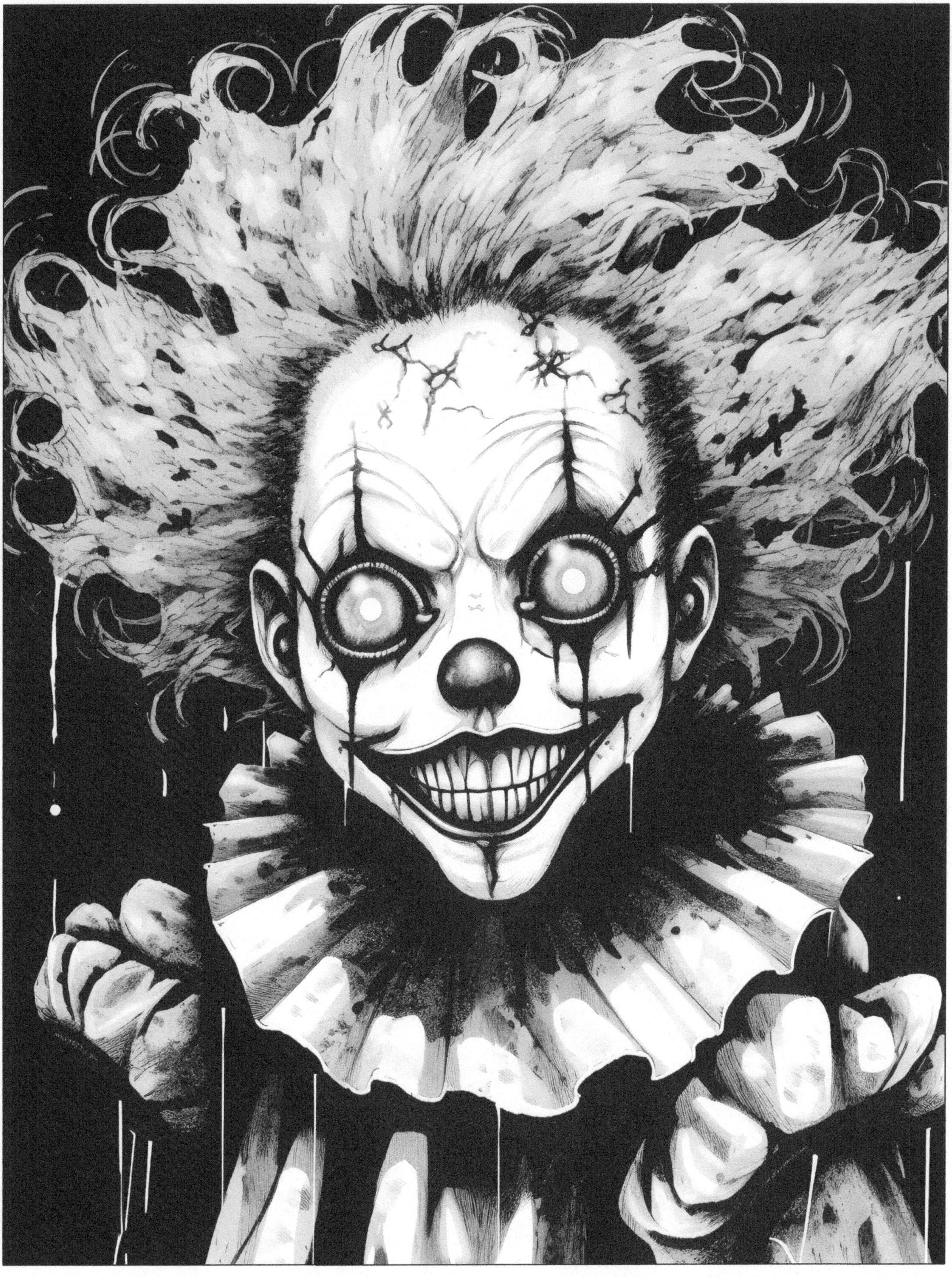

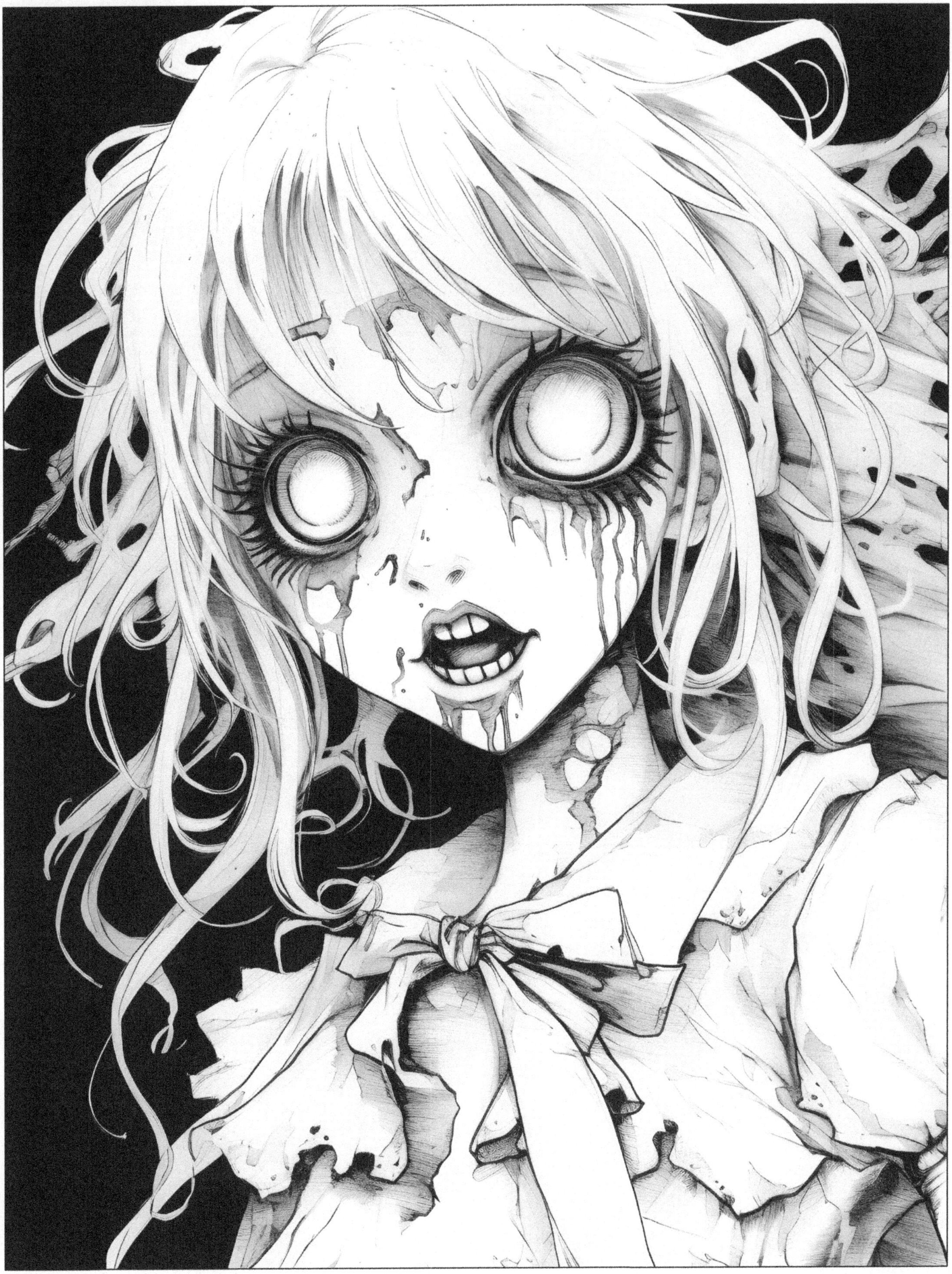

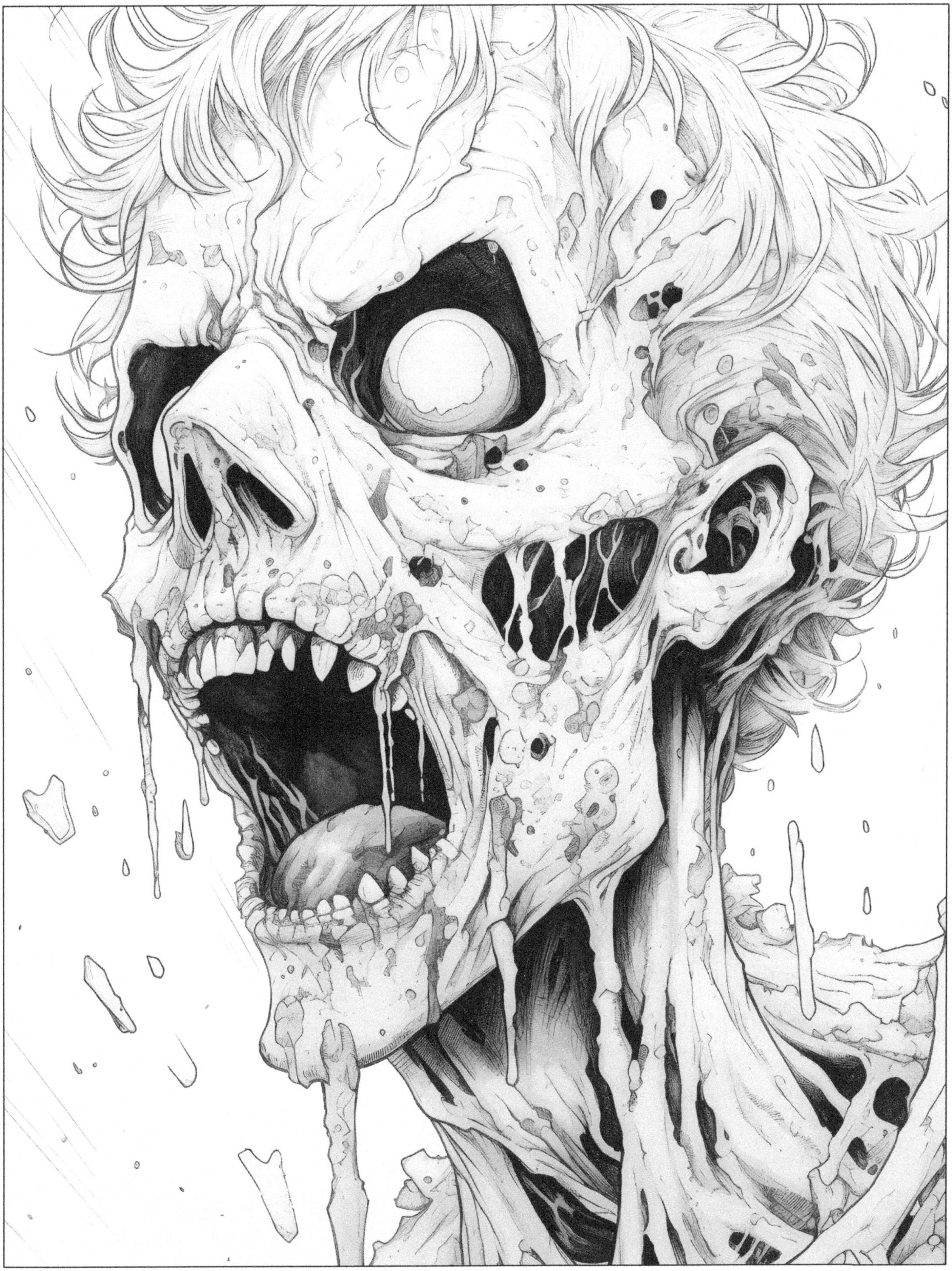

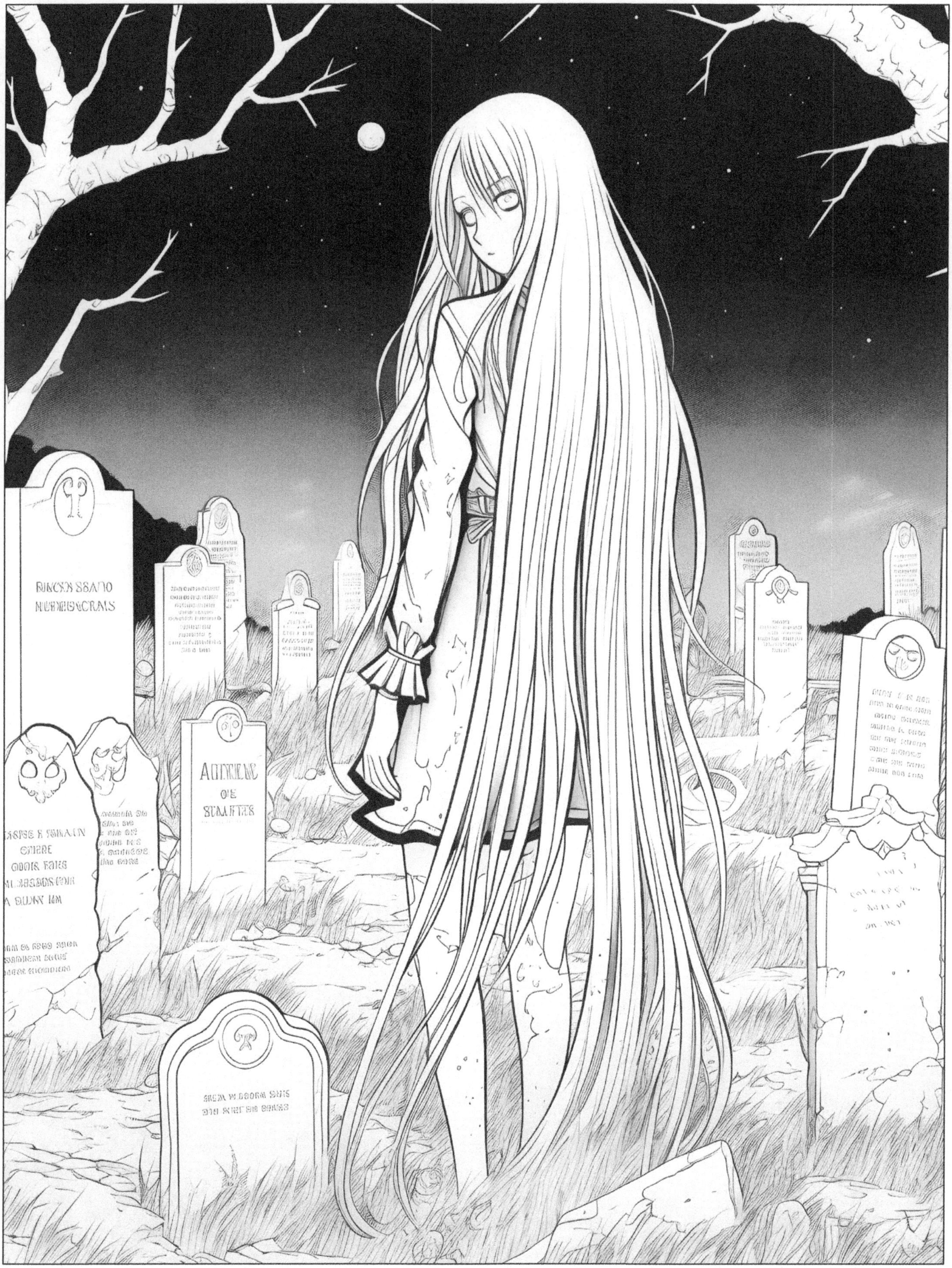

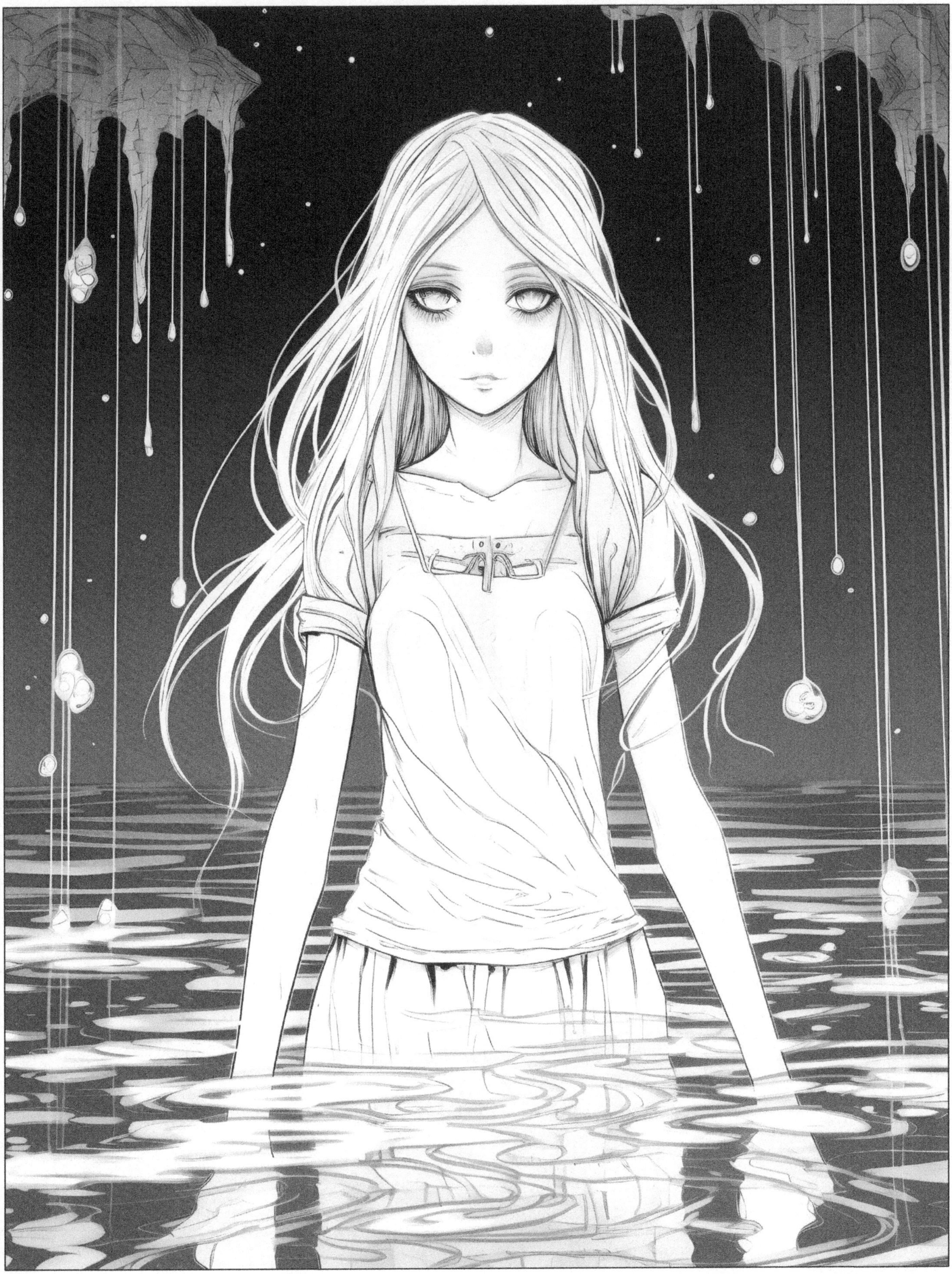

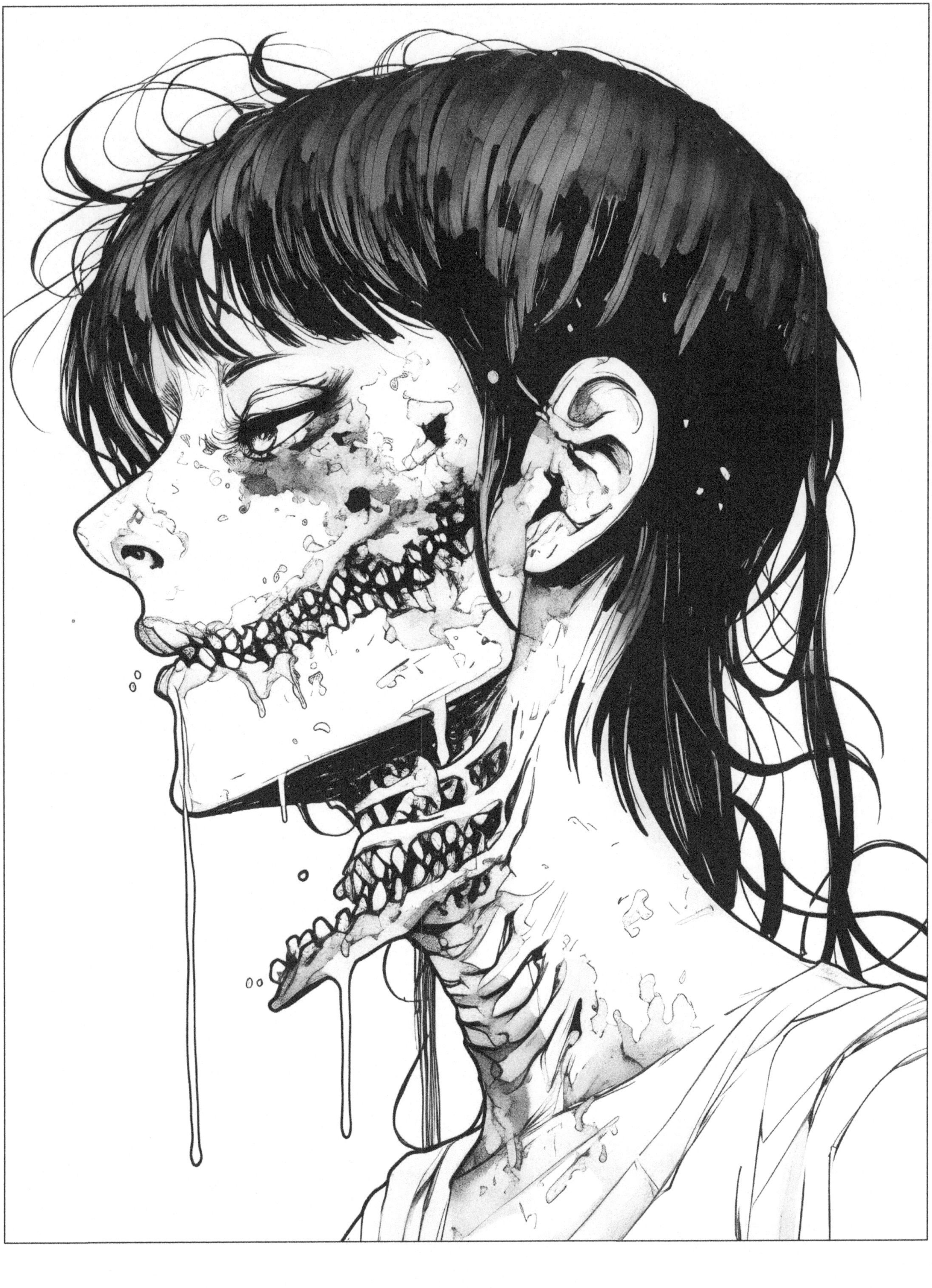

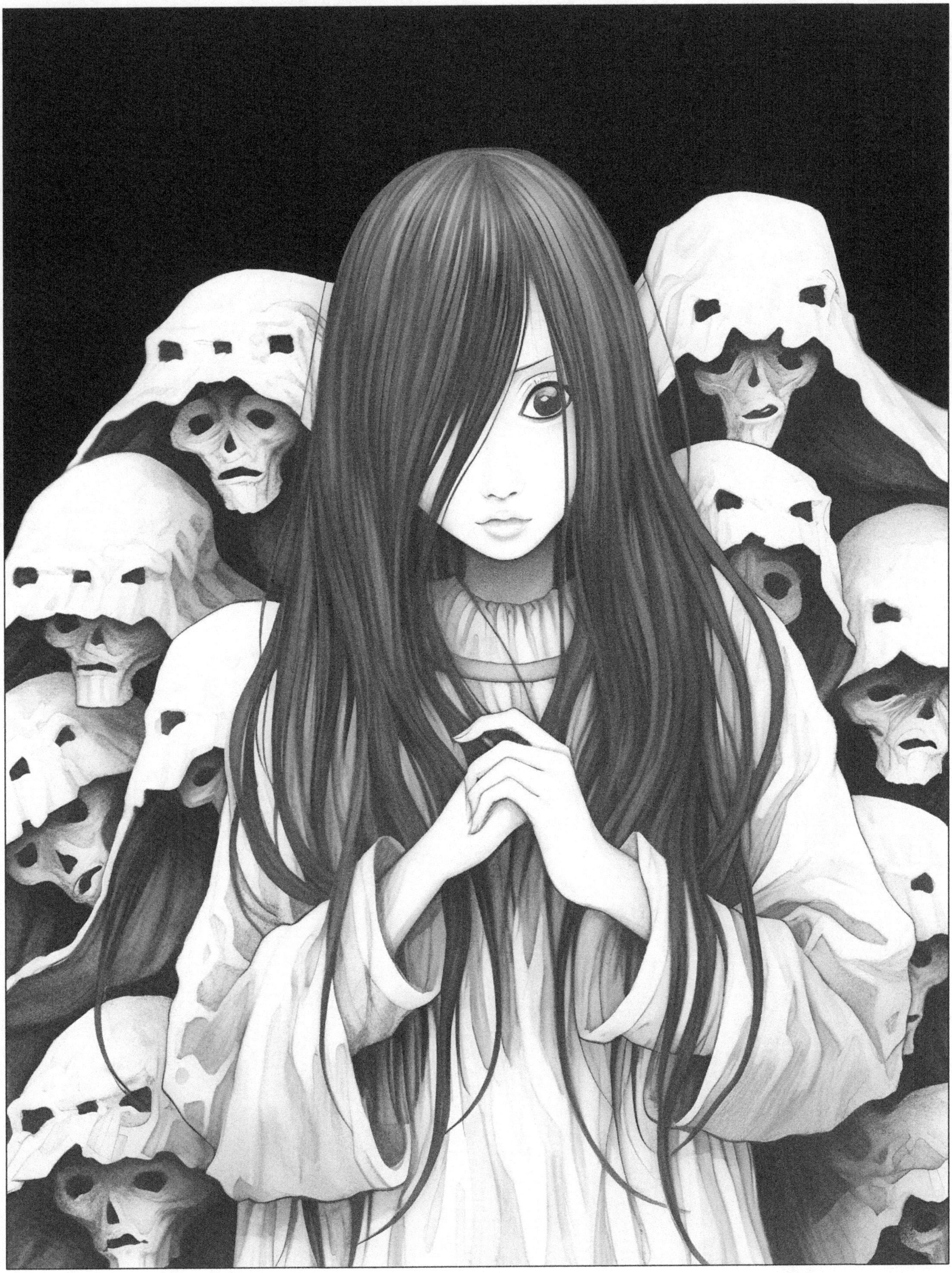

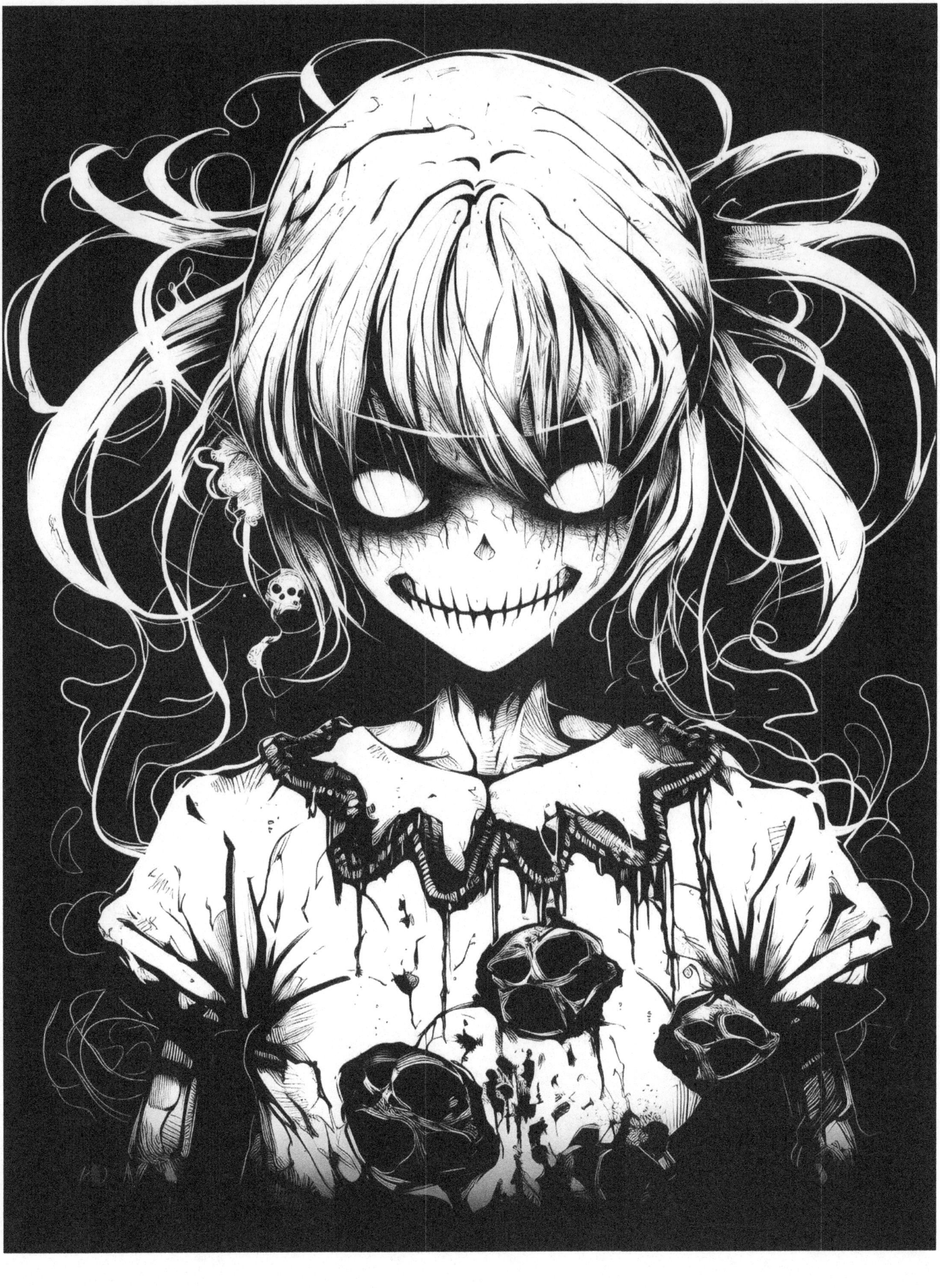

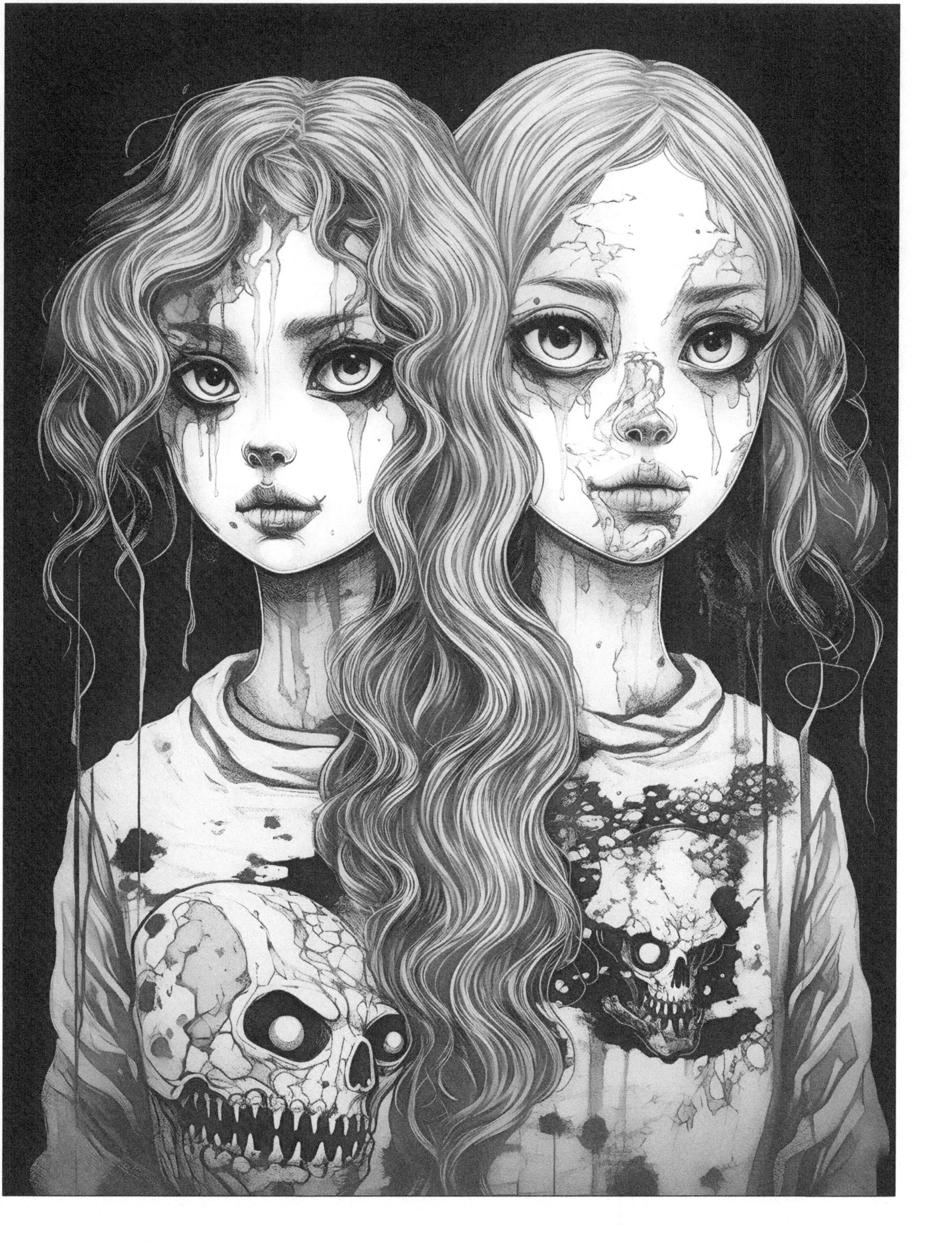

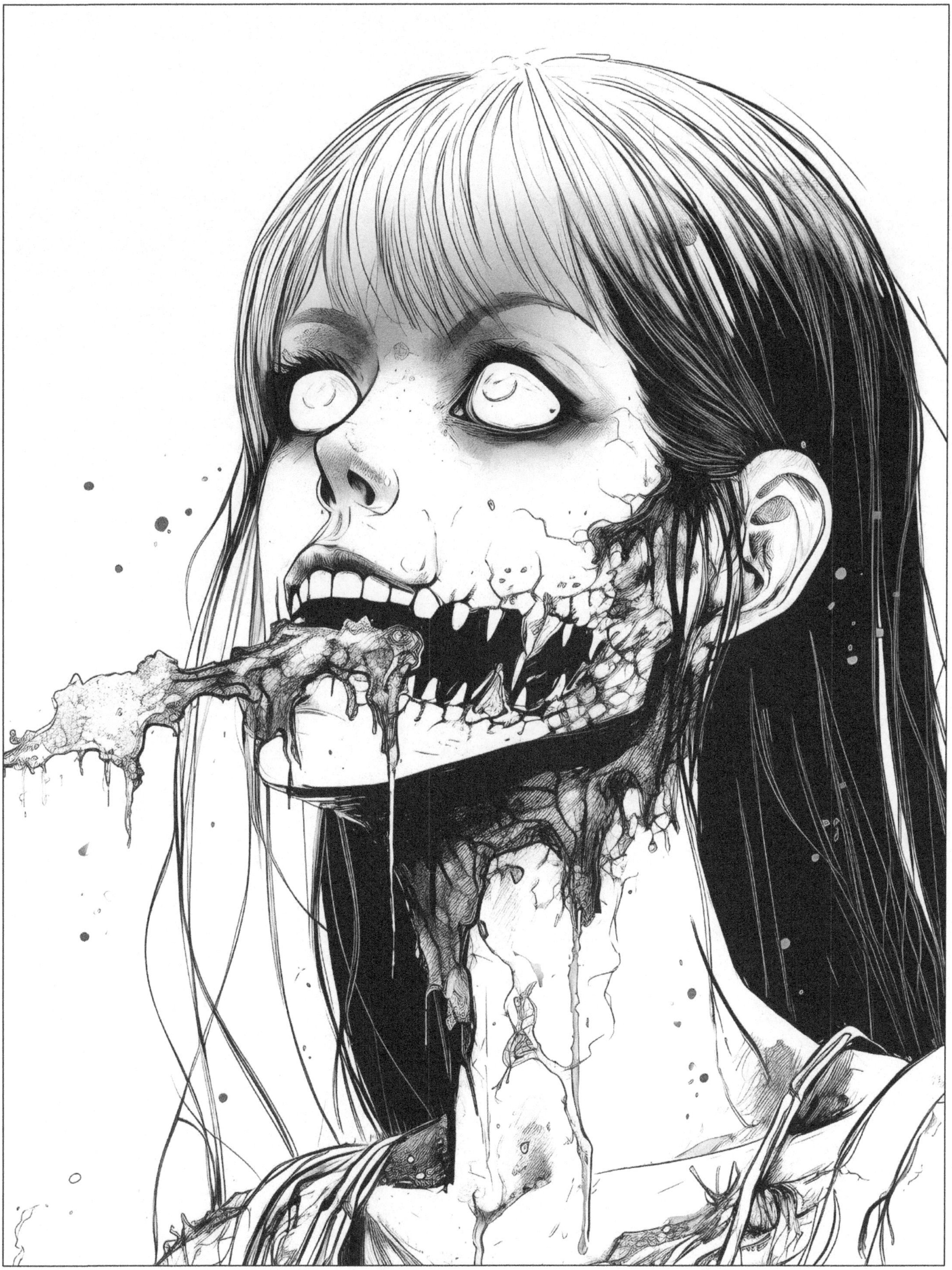

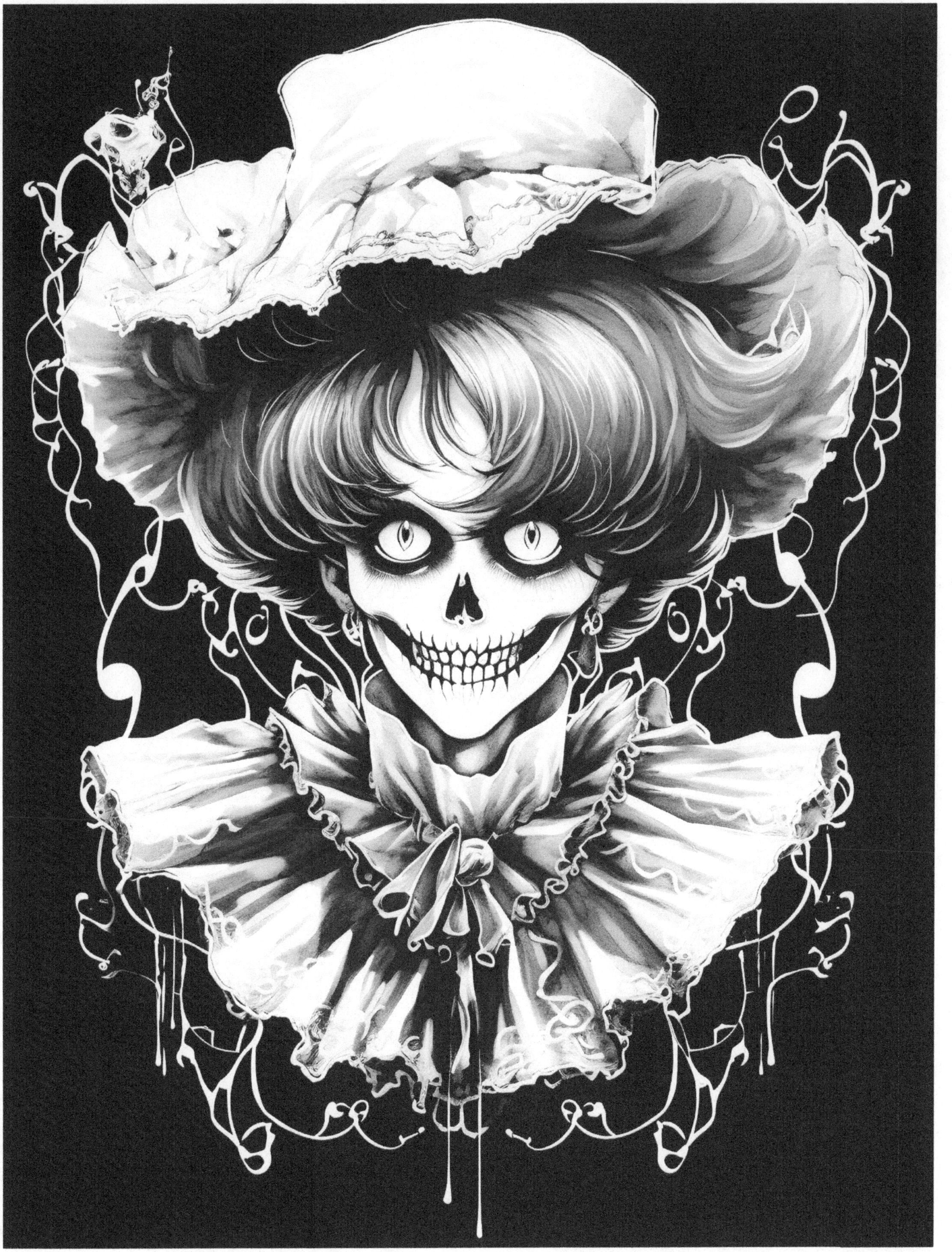

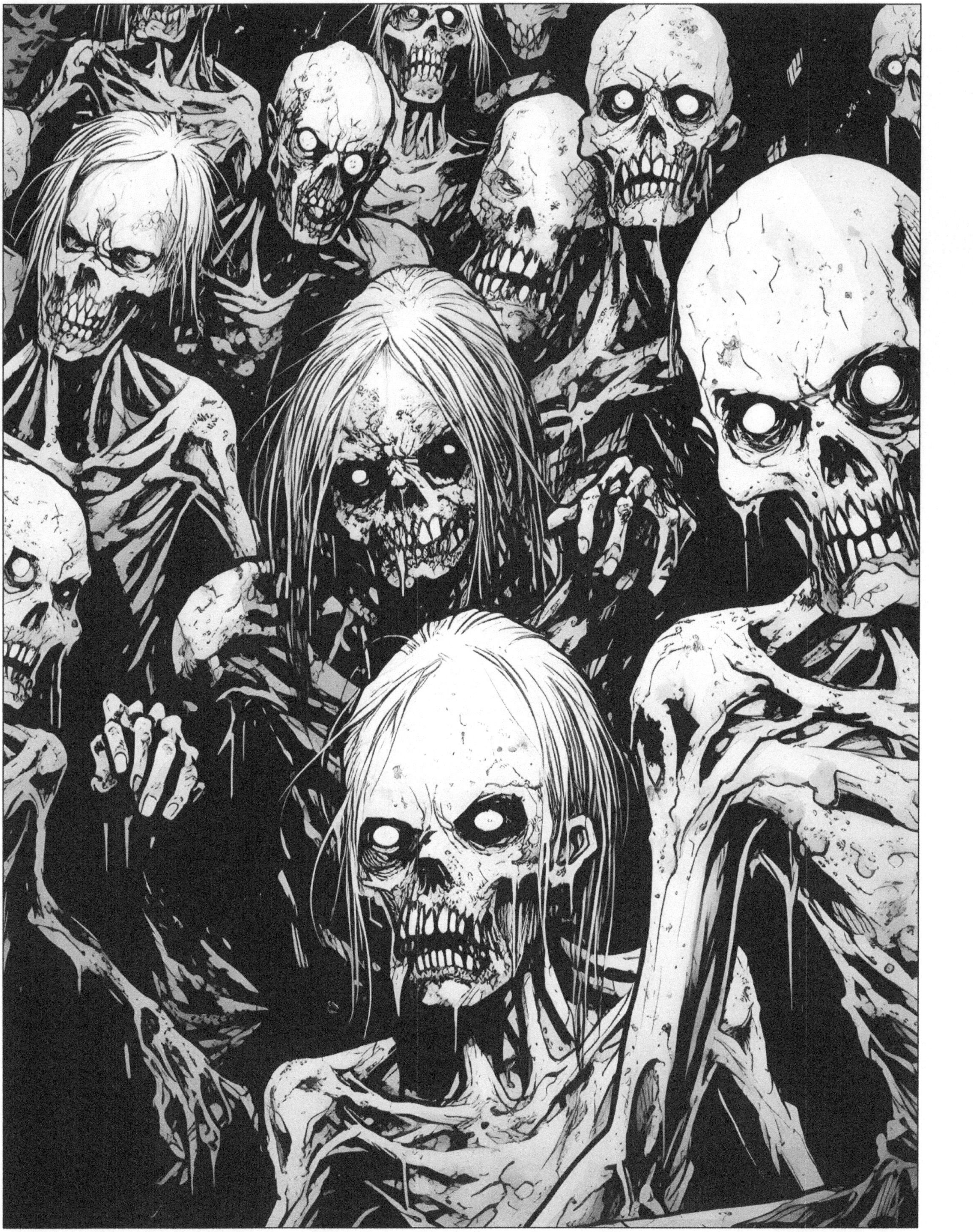

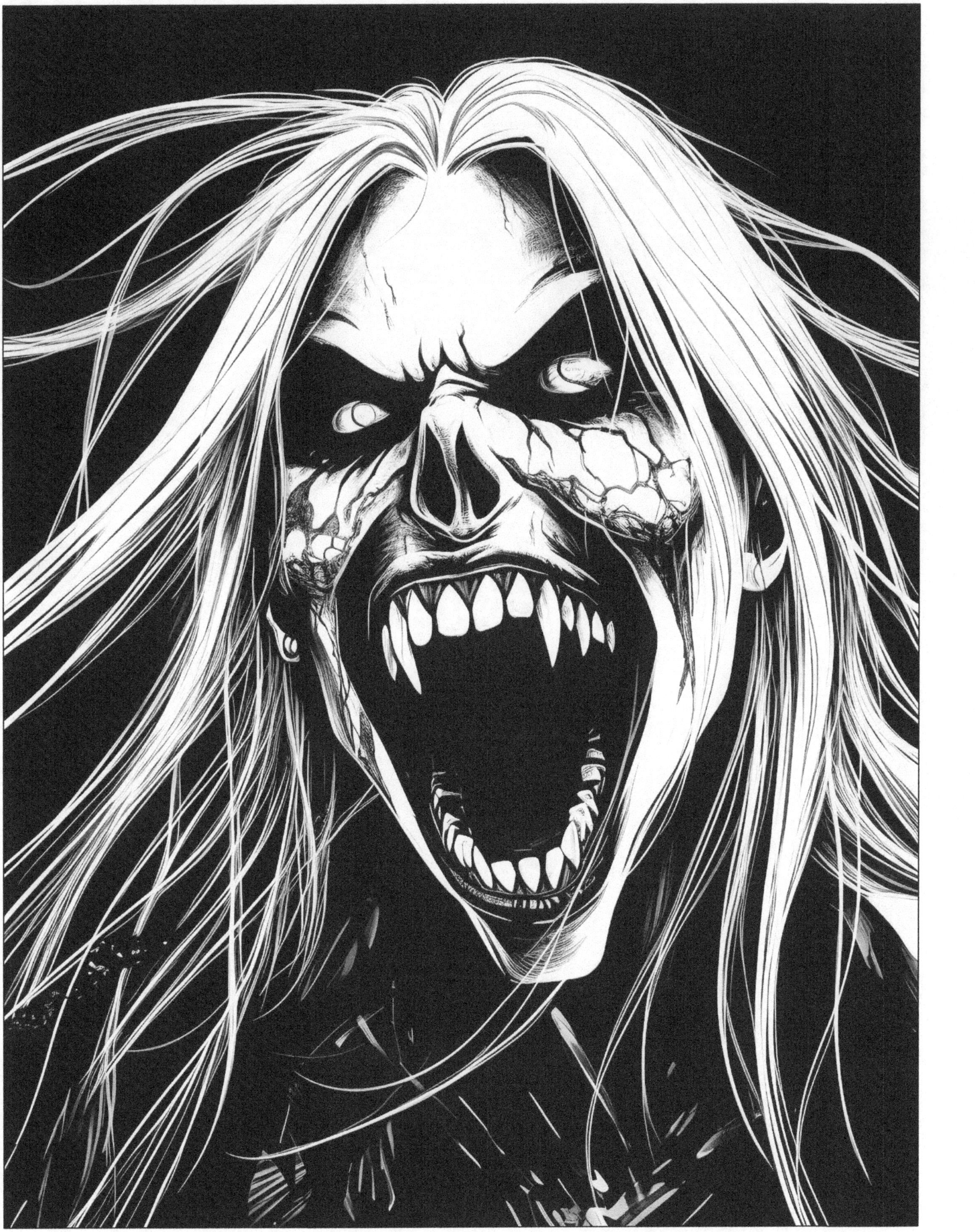

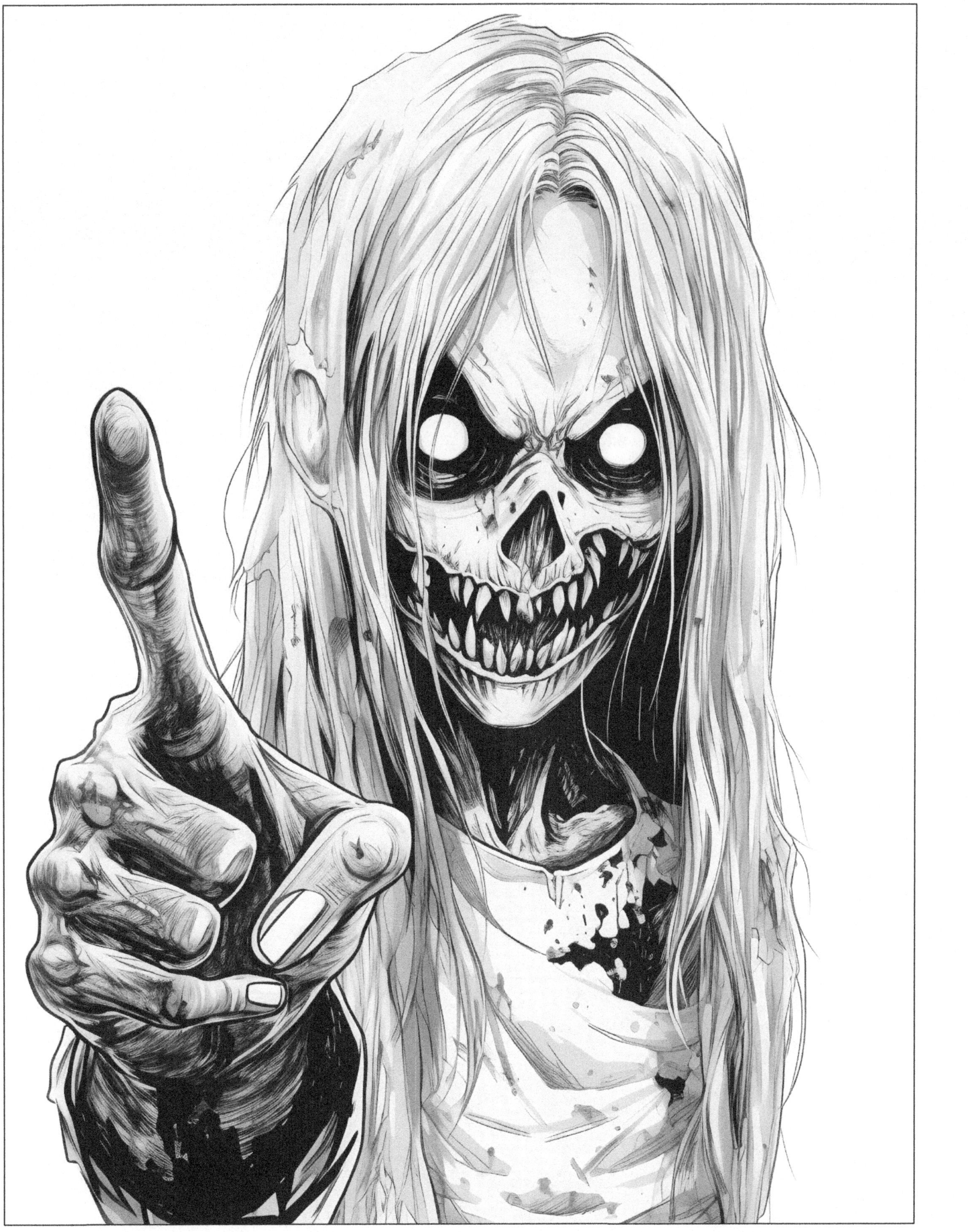

Made in United States
North Haven, CT
01 October 2023

42232376R00059